Go Vegan Once A Week

How To Become And Stay Vegan
Using The Oaw Formula
A Healthy Guide To A Plant Based
And An Animal Friendly Life

BRAD MEIER

ISBN 978-9-69-239232-7

www.saturneditors.com/bradmeier

Table of Contents

Introduction

Do You Understand What You Want?

Many people think about strict dieting when they consider veganism. They believe they must have a strict meal plan to be a vegan. However, that is not entirely what veganism is about. To become a vegan, you have to change your lifestyle. Usually, most humans have a carnivorous or omnivorous diet; leaving those diets and becoming vegan should be thoroughly considered. You must understand what you are going in for, the lifestyle you will drop, and everything attached to the new lifestyle.

It is not out of normalcy when people relate veganism to a rigorous process. People who advise others to imbibe the vegan lifestyle usually make it seem stressful with many unpalatable recipes and stern warnings about the dangers of mixing veganism with other types of diets. Becoming a vegan starts feeling like enrolling to serve in the army.

Practicing veganism doesn't have to be tedious like that. If it is a lifestyle that becomes tedious, it ceases to be a lifestyle but a chore. There are so many reasons people might want to go into veganism; whatever the reason, the process should not be stressful. It should be an exciting experience anyone can be willing to embark on.

Those who are prepared to begin veganism halt their decisions for many reasons. They might love the whole idea of being a vegan and the benefits it brings to them; however, they might also be concerned about the health detriments. No matter the importance of an action, it might not be carried out if it poses some threat. Many people fear the adverse effects it might have on their health. If people begin veganism to ensure they live healthier lives, an adverse effect of the lifestyle will be counterproductive on their journey.

The most concern on the health detriments is due to the abrupt change in diet. Abruptly changing a thing can be stressful and, in most cases, might not work. This is why some people halt between beginning veganism and ignoring the process. They spend time pondering whether veganism is worth risking their health for. They wonder if they should walk into their kitchen, throw away every animal product, and start a vegan diet immediately. It is imperative to understand that veganism does not work that way. If it were that way, there would not be veganism. People might not come clean about how they practice theirs, so you might feel everyone practiced it strictly in their first few tries.

Some other concerns might be about the social impact it will have on them. Changing a formerly carnivorous or omnivorous diet to a vegan one can become hard to cope with socially. It makes it seem like the person has suddenly become a picky eater. Their friends begin to lose access to sharing a meal with them because there is an abrupt change in meals, followed by intense scrutiny of the ingredients used in every cooked meal. It becomes worse when it is hard to find meals that suit their vegan needs in a public gathering. The change in diet also affects grocery shopping. There is an idea that vegans must be careful of the constituents of the food products they buy. It is quite hard these days to decipher foods without animal products from foods that are. There has to be thorough research on brands that are strictly vegan in their constituents and not just vegan in name.

This can be overwhelming for a person that wishes to begin. They think of the stress they will go through researching brands and products that will be healthy for their new lifestyle. In a world full of stress, they begin to imagine how they can manage life stress and prolonged grocery shopping time. A person that might have programmed twenty minutes of grocery shopping might end up spending two hours with barely any grocery item to show for the time spent.

Some also consider how sustainable it is for a beginner. Anyone might say the process is sustainable because they see other people practice it for years or have practiced it. However, it might not appear that way to a person at the beginning phase. They will have thoughts about themselves, wondering if they get fed up and the probability of returning to where they started. These thoughts are not wrong because getting fed up with a stressful process is normal.

These are fears and demotivators that stem from a misconception of the process. To begin a process, you have to understand it in its depths. Without understanding, you might not be able to enjoy and immerse yourself wholly in this. There is no progressive way to understand the dynamics and tricks of how you can practice veganism sustainably, have social relevance and still maintain good health than reading this book. This book will lead you on tour to understand the nooks and crannies of veganism and how to practice it flexibly.

Chapter 1
What Matters?

To truly understand veganism, it is vital to understand the meaning and why it is an ethical choice. If you don't understand these, you might miss out on your reason for choosing veganism. These will also make you understand if you truly understand the term and are ready to begin a gradual lifestyle change. Understanding this will also lead you to understand if you made the right choice by being vegan or if the lifestyle is not for you. Even though the world is encouraged to imbibe this lifestyle, it is truthfully not for everyone. Veganism is not a lifestyle that a person has to be forced into. They have to deliberately choose if it will be a solution to their problem. If a person is forced into veganism, it might be practiced to the extreme. At this point, it ceases to be practiced because it has become something that provokes fear in the heart of the person practicing. This eludes veganism from its true meaning, which includes a practice of choice. Subsequently, you will understand the meaning of veganism, so you can see your weigh your options better and understand the advantage of choosing to be a vegan.

Meaning of becoming a vegan

To understand what becoming a vegan entails, you must be aware of veganism's meaning. When people hear of veganism, they believe it is a person that does not eat animal products and their derivatives. However, veganism is more than that. Veganism is so broad that it is not limited only to food but also essential daily items like clothes, soap, and every item you can think of. Veganism is a lifestyle that encourages using only plant-based products, including clothes, foods, and other essentials. It also includes the avoidance of the use of animals for pleasure purposes.

In straightforward terms, veganism is defined as a lifestyle that practicably excludes all cruelty and exploitation of animals for selfish interests like food or entertainment. It also encompasses the development of animal-free ways to improve human, animal, and environmental wellbeing.

There are many ways a person can embrace a vegan lifestyle. They might not be scientists to ensure all testing is done without using animals. However, they can only try what is within their reach. No matter the kind of vegan a person is, they abstain from animal derivatives like meat, animal milk, fish, butter, cheese, and clothes made from animals. They ensure that they maintain a strictly plant-based diet.

As a vegan, you can choose to be flexitarian or strictly vegan. A flexitarian might have animal products like honey from bees and some other animal products once in a while; meanwhile, a strict vegan will have no animal produce or item produced from animal forced labor.

Veganism is a new world, different from the omnivorous diet that most people enjoy. Becoming a vegan means that you will have to replace those nutrients that are obtained from meat with plant-based foods. Now, this might seem like a hassle: these animal products from which these nutrients are readily found in stores more than the vegan sources.

Nutrients like calcium are needed for many body functions, including aiding the absorption of other minerals, giving strength to the teeth and bones, and aiding muscle contraction. Calcium is mainly found in dairy products like milk, which are animal products. Since there will be a diet change to vegan type, there will be a change from dairy milk to plant-based milk fortified with calcium. Similarly, vitamin D and B_{12} are obtained mainly from animal sources, but supplements can replace them. Similarly, an omega-3 fatty acid that is obtained chiefly from salmon can be replaced by supplements. There is an initial frustration about the change in sources of the usual nutrients from animals, but eventually, the process will become easier.

When people encourage people to become vegans, they use the calorie deficit and healthy eating arguments. However, that is not a hundred percent valid. A vegan can eat a very unhealthy diet and gain more weight than before they began the lifestyle. If you are choosing veganism to lose weight, it will be imperative to weigh your options and consider the type of foods you will eat as a vegan.

Carbs are needed for energy but are the primary source of excess weight. Truthfully, a vegan diet contains a considerable amount of carbs and can be counterproductive to your vegan health journey if you don't understand the dynamics.

History of veganism

You cannot explain a term thoroughly without understanding how it started. Veganism cannot be talked about without the inclusion of a vegetarian diet. Some people confuse the two terms because they are very close in meaning. In the start, vegetarianism was used to refer to a vegetable diet. However, in subsequent years, there was a modification of the definition. A vegetarian diet is a plant-based diet that includes dairy products like milk, cheese, butter, and honey. In simpler terms, a vegetarian is a person who eats vegetables and fruits and uses other animal derivatives, except eating the animal's meat. A vegan was hence referred to as a strict vegetarian, preventing itself from using animal products.

The earliest forms of vegetarianism can be traced back to 3300 to 1300 B.C. in western and northern India. A handful of notable Indian philosophers, poets, and emperors imbibed this diet lifestyle. Since the name 'vegan' was not coined then, it is unclear what type of vegetarianism these people practiced. Throughout history, some notable Greeks and Romans also imbibed this lifestyle, most of which were significant literary figures. These names might not be mentioned because there might be no familiarity between their names and who they are.

A notable Greek philosopher and mathematician known for his theories—Pythagoras- was said to have practiced strict vegetarianism in his time. Although there was no name for it, he was very particular about what he ate and wore. It is believed that he was among the first people that advocated for strict vegetarianism in his time. Still, there are some controversies surrounding this because of his enigmatic life. There was no specific explanation for why and how he lived and made his followers live. Philosophers like Plato and others who came in close contact with him described him as one who lived a pure life and avoided killing people who kill. His life was so cryptic that he avoided hunters as well as cooks. He and his followers avoided wool since it was gotten from sheep. He and his followers also avoided beans, which makes philosophers wonder if he avoided all he did purely because of his vegetarianism or other reasons.

Despite how unclear Pythagoras' stance was on strict vegetarianism, there are still some notable people of that time that practiced this lifestyle. A prominent person that practiced it is Al-ma' are, an Arab poet. His practice of strict vegetarianism was because of the health and humane benefits. He believed that humans needed to imbibe this lifestyle to ensure the transmigration of their souls, as well as compassion for animals. He openly believed that animals deserved compassion like humans. He believed there should be no difference in the compassion given to these two groups.

The movement gained increased recognition in U.S. and Britain in the 1800s, when there were more people curious about the lifestyle, as well as people who practiced it publicly and were willing to release publications to the populace to educate them on what it was about. Although people were beginning to be informed about it and were willing to adopt the lifestyle, only a few people followed the lifestyle strictly. A publication was released in 1813, titled 'A vindication for a natural diet,' by Percy Shelly, aimed at abolishing the use of animals as meat and strong wine. Two years later, a London physician – William lamb, will support his view by expressing his belief in the potency of vegetables and water.

Lambe believed in good health by eating lots of vegetables and abstaining from meat. He was linked to strict vegetarianism because he believed meat and other dairy products were unnecessary for man's wellbeing. According to him, his plant-based diet can manage small and significant illnesses. He also believed that meat and other dairy products are tied together. A person can choose to eat meat and dairy products or not. The essential thing involved is if they eat meat, they should also eat dairy products. If they do not eat meat, they should have nothing to do with other dairy products. In the 30s of the 19th century, graham's meatless diet was formed by Sylvester graham. This diet was popular in the U.S. because it was believed to function as a health remedy. The diet was solely on homemade bread from stone-ground flour; the rest comprised fruits, vegetables, and water.

As the popularity of veganism increased, more organizations were created to support the movement. Some notable groups were concordium, temple school, and Fruitland, which were notable creations that helped spread the word about veganism in Britain. Amos Alcott founded the temple school and Fruitland in 1834 and 1843, respectively, while James Pierrepoint created Concordium in the Alcott house. These were notable beginnings of the vegan movement, although it still hadn't gotten its name.

As the movement began with the Alcott family in Britain, it continued succeeding till they created another organization. The foreign and British society for abstinence from animal food and humanity promotion was created in 1843 and governed by a wealthy benefactor of their house, Sophia Chichester. The family was active in the vegetarian movement; they also helped establish the U.K. vegetarian society, and the organization held its first meeting in 1884.

Since the name vegan was not yet coined, they separated vegans from other vegetarian practitioners by referring to them as strict vegetarians. The others were referred to as the less strict kind of vegetarian. Most vegetarians at that time and in notable organizations practiced the less strict type.

As time went on, more strict vegetarians (vegans) emerged. In 1851 a popular magazine known as vegetarian messenger released a publication that backed strict vegetarianism. In this publication, alternative solutions to shoe leather were discussed, which showed some vegetarians rejected the use of animals for several selfish human purposes and not only for food. A popular publication released in 1886 titled a plea for vegetarianism by henry salt explained that not all vegetarians use dairy products in their meals. The Hygeian Home cookbook written by Rusell Tralls is the first American vegan cookbook, and it was published in 1874. Although it was referred to as a vegetarian cookbook at the time, it is clear that the book is vegan through a close modern cross-examination. It incorporated several vegetables and crops without using dairy products, yeast, salt, sugar, acids, grease, alkalies, or other condiments. Subsequently, more recipe books were released; a notable one was 'No animal food' released by Rupert Wheldon in 1910, which also excluded the use of dairy products while cooking. All these publications, including individual mindset, had caused little controversy. The vegetarians believed that the practice of vegetarianism without including dairy products was impracticable. This points toward the opposition to veganism by most vegetarians, especially when taking milk.

Mahatma Gandhi joined the vegetarian society and was an executive during his stay in London. During his speech in one of their meetings, he shared his idea on vegetarianism: it was tied to health purposes and the ethics of animal preservation. The lactovegetarian understood the ethics attached to veganism but believed that veganism was unattainable and a stumbling block to the vegetarian spread.

Veganism did not get its name till the 20th century. The idea of veganism kept being turned down by many people but was embraced by a few individuals. In the 40s, some members of the vegetarian society requested a part of the newsletter to be dedicated to non-dairy vegetarians, which was rejected by the society. Although the request was rejected, Leicester's branch secretary, Donald Watson, created a quarterly newsletter titled the vegan news. Donald and Dorothy created the word vegan. According to them, the word 'vegan' was based on the last two and first three letters of vegetarian. According to Watson, it was the end and beginning of vegetarianism. In this newsletter, they asked readers if they thought of anything better to represent non-dairy vegetarians. There were several suggestions, but no one was better fitting than vegan.

After the creation vegan newsletter, the movement spread to more people, with its edition attracting more than a hundred letters, a notable one from George S. Bernard. He said he'd give up his diary and eggs. The vegan society held its meeting in November, which turned out to be celebrated every year as the vegan month, specifically November 1st. As the movement increased in its reach, more books were written. The vegan newsletter published a vegan list containing animal-free products, including toothpaste, glue, stationery, and shoe polishing. As the movement continued, they soon clarified their stance on using other animal products. Watson discouraged using animals for any products, not exclusively for diet. According to him, it was a superstitious belief that human life depended on animals, especially because animals have the same feelings as us. He advocated for people to live without the exploitation of animals. In subsequent years, the vice president of the vegan society founded the plant milk society, which became a widely distributed and used soy milk in western countries. Catherine Nimmo and Rubin Abramowitz founded the first vegan society in America, which linked the lifestyle to no harm.

Types of veganism

Even though veganism is central for people who despise the exploitation of animals for food and other practices, there are different types of vegans. There are four main types of veganism that people might practice, namely,

- Health veganism
- Ethical veganism
- Environmental veganism
- Feminists' veganism
- Religious veganism

Health veganism

Health vegans are the vegans who give up animal food solely because of health reasons. Many people join the veganism movement and imbibe the lifestyle because they believe it will improve their health in the long run. Some research has shown that vegans have lower body mass index and reduced risk of cancers. Since this book is not directed toward the health implications of veganism, it will be left out of the explanation. The bottom line is that health vegans only care about what they can gain 'health-wise' from the process.

Ethical veganism

Ethical vegans are the vegans that give up animal food solely because it is against ethics. These vegans believe that animals have feelings; if they have feelings like humans, it will be wrong to mistreat them. As an animal is killed to be cooked, it goes through so much pain, just like a human going through pain before death, and as such, it is unethical to eat them. These vegans also believe that if humans cannot subject themselves to harsh labor or behavior that is solely pleasing to another human and displeasing to themselves, why should animals do so? If humans cannot plow fields endlessly, it is unethical for animals to do so. Also, some extremists of this group believe that people should not keep animals as pets because it is discomforting to the pets. Apart from Health vegans, this group is also a prevalent type of people in veganism.

Environmental veganism

This type of vegans is vegans because they believe that veganism is a move that promotes a more sustainable environment. The world is an ecosystem with different organisms coexisting with each other. Destroying the lineage of an organism can cause an unbalance in nature. In the environmental vegan's beliefs, if a man stops eating animals and exploiting them for their interests, more animals will be in the ecosystem to bring about a balance. Sustaining animals will also avoid multiple extinction of several notable species. Even though the specie is not popular, it should not be eaten or exploited since it might have an essential role in the ecosystem.

Feminist veganism

This is the least popular type of veganism that is tied to the movement of feminism. A handful of people started this movement, which has been around for more than half a century. These people believe that feminism is closely tied to veganism.

Religious veganism

This veganism is borne from a religious standpoint. As there are several religions in the world, many beliefs also differ. Although this type of veganism is practiced based on the demands of a particular religion, it can be backed by ethical, health, or environmental veganism. Some religions believe that veganism is vital for a person's physical and spiritual health. Meanwhile, others might tie veganism to ethical beliefs and the compassion of God for all creatures. Some also believe that veganism is vital for the world to be in balance. Whatsoever the belief of the religion might be, it is imperative to note that the belief is solely tied to the religion they practice.

Things you will be giving up as a vegan

Vegans abstain from animal food, clothing made from animals, and generally, any action that will cause animal suffering. As a vegan, you will be giving up so much, but considering the benefits attached will be worth it. This book specifies these products so that you might not be confused about vegan-specific things.

Meat

Giving up meat is a thing that vegans and vegetarians have in common. As a vegan, you have to abstain from every kind of meat. There are no specific meats that are advisable for vegans. As a vegan, you have to give up every type of animal meat, including chickens and cows. Even though you will give up meats, some substitutes are suitable for you and will make you forget the chicken you used to have regularly.

Animal seafood

Some people think that as vegans, some animal seafood is permitted. Veganism discourages anything that causes pain for the animal. As a vegan, you can decide to eat seaweed and other seafood that are not from animals. No matter how little the sea animal is, it would be best if you thought about doing away with it as a vegan.

Eggs and diary

This is part of the reasons why vegans differ from vegetarians. A vegetarian might say eggs and dairy do not kill the animal. They might be correct, but the truth is even though it does not kill the animal immediately, it makes the animal suffer and reduces its lifespan of the animals. All dairy products should be avoided as a vegan, including cheese, butter, margarine, and milk. No matter the shade the dairy product takes, it should be avoided. Vegans also look for ingredients in food items to ensure that eggs and dairy products are not included.

Animal-made clothing

Using animals to make different types of clothing has become a norm in society, like a worm interwoven with silk. Almost all brands make their clothing and shoes from animals. It becomes like a man cannot do without animals for this purpose. This situation is what veganism aims to abolish. The use of animals for clothing brings stress to the animal and kills them. Clothing items like leather and wool are top-rated in the clothing industry in making items from luxury to basic. Many animal products are used to make clothes like silk, animal dyes, wool, and other kinds of animal skin. As a vegan, you will be doing away with all of that.

Toiletries

This might be surprising to some people who don't know the process and ingredients of toiletry making. Most toiletries are made from animals. The concept of toiletry making from animals can be easily understood because these animal parts are more readily available than others. People making toiletry do not buy or rear an animal for the sole purpose of toiletry making. They use the parts of the animal for meat and other parts for other essentials; then, the rest is used for toiletry. This means animal toiletries are usually cheaper than others because their constituents are cheaper. For example, most soaps are made from tallow. Tallow is a part of animal fat. After these animals are used for several purposes, the leftover fats are used to make soap.

Another example is collagen derived from glycerine, obtained from animals and used to make toothpaste, hair care products, soaps, moisturizers, and shaving foams. It is used in these products because it acts as a lubricant. Sheep wool's lanolin is used chiefly for moisturizers and lip balm. Animal-derived stearic acid is also one of the animal-based products used in toiletries; it is used chiefly in shaving foam, face creams, and shampoos. Many other products are derived from animals, like lactic acid and allantoin, used in moisturizers and kinds of toothpaste, respectively.

Insect food and products

As a vegan, you will also give up insect foods. These insect foods are foods made from edible worms and edible fried insects. Every person does not eat these foods. However, if you eat them, you have to do away with them. There are animal products that have been a source of controversy for years in the vegan community—honey. Many vegans believe that it is unfair to take honey because the bees are reared for commercial purposes. Meanwhile, others believe it is ethical to take honey since it doesn't hurt the bees. A vegan might or might not take honey, depending on their stance on this subject.

Animal labor and unethical animal use

Depending on the type of veganism you practice, you will have to do away with unlawful animal practices. One of these practices is using animals as labor on farms and other areas. If you use animals in your fields, it might be time to get an appropriate instrument to plow your fields and do your work. If you cannot do it, you should not think it is ethical for an animal to do it. Similarly, using animals for unethical testing should be a practice you abhor.

Correctness of choice

You might wonder if being vegan is worth the trouble, especially because many other vegetarian options are open to you; you wonder if you're making the right choice. If you weigh the options available, it is clear that you made the best choice. Although you might not see the dividends of your choice immediately, in the long run, you will thank yourself. Being vegan benefits the practicer, other people, animals, and the planet. Below are some benefits that veganism has on different aspects of life.

Self-benefits

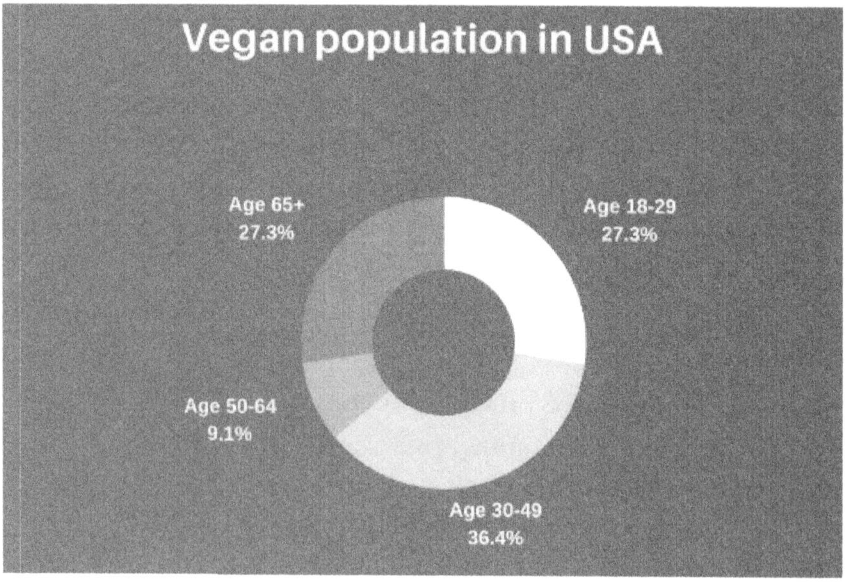

As a person, many benefits being a vegan will give you. The most crucial benefit is healthier eating, which is beneficial to your body mass index as well as the total health of your body. The health benefits are a significant reason that draws people into veganism. As a vegan, you will also have a clear conscience while eating. It is not worth it to eat while thinking about the animals that died in making the dish you are consuming. As a vegan, your heart will be more at rest while you eat because you know that you didn't only save the lives of the animals but also saved them from suffering. Vegans are happier because of the lives they save with their diets.

Benefits of veganism to other non-veganism

It might seem weird to hear, but veganism has positive effects even on those who are not practicing. Usually, vegans save 200 animals annually through lifesaving practices and animal labor abstinence. This means that even though non-vegans don't believe in this, this practice preserves animals for everyone. This is not the only benefit that veganism has on other people.

Today the world is faced with hunger. Through recession and inflation, many people are not able to afford food. People believe this situation cannot be helped but can only be reversed by the philanthropic gestures of well-meaning people. This might be true, but not entirely because veganism combats world hunger. It might not seem plausible since you believe you are only saving the animals when you don't eat them. Do you know that farmers give more food to the livestock they rear than humans? This means choosing to be a vegan reduces the number of animals reared. Because if there is no increase in demand for the animals, the farmer will not increase the animals they rear. This will lead to a decrease in the animal food supply, making more food available to humans.

Another essential benefit of veganism is the water-conserving benefits. Being a vegan means that you will save water for other people. This might not seem to add up either, but it is true. It takes more water to feed an animal than the amount it takes to water a crop. Comparing these two variables, you will understand that water will increase if the amount used to feed the livestock is reduced. As vegans do not eat meat, there would be a reduction in livestock rearing for consumption leading to a decrease in water use. Also, it is universally known that meat eaters drink more water than people on plant-based diets. This is because plant foods already have a sizable amount of water. Plant foods contain more water than meat; a vegan will be less thirsty than a meat eater. This also entails that vegans provide water for other people.

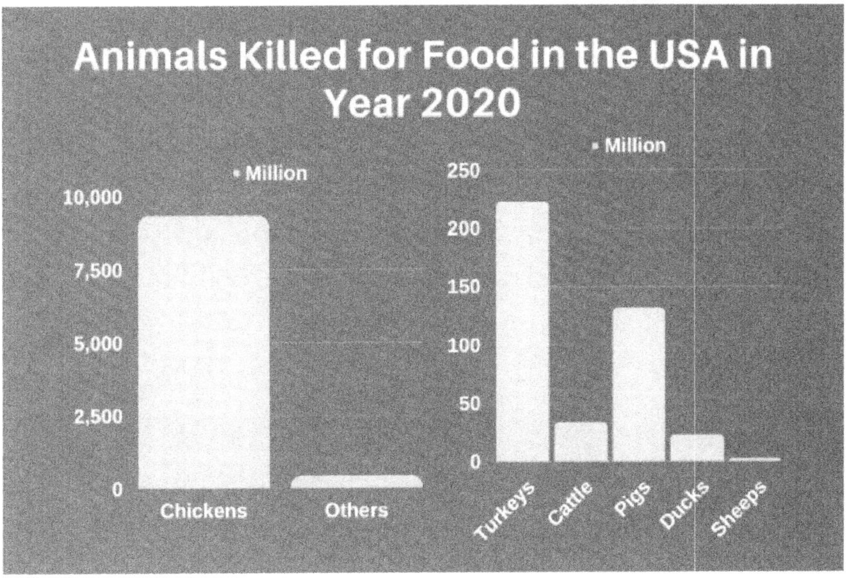

Benefits of veganism to animals

Before going on to other benefits that veganism gives to animals, it is imperative to talk about the life preservation it gives to these animals. To eat the meat of an animal, you have to kill the animal first. There is no way to get an animal's meat without killing it. Vegans are against eating meat, a lifesaving method for animals. Apart from the meat aspect, most animals are used in commercial settings as labor and for other commercial purposes. These animals are kept in a tight space, with no room for excess movement in these settings. Their movements are restricted so much that they do not get to go out of their shed. The ones that leave the shed are big enough animals. In similar settings, the male chicks hatched are killed since their growth will not be as fast as their female counterparts. Also, they kill them because they will not lay eggs which means they are useless to the farm. Multiple pregnancies are initiated in cows to bring new calves for consumption and milk purposes. The calves brought to the world through forceful and initiated pregnancies do not have access to the milk for more than a few days before the farm packages the milk for humans. Fishes are killed and taken out of their habitats to private ponds where they can be reared for slaughter. The list shows that it can never be ethical to rear animals for selfish reasons.

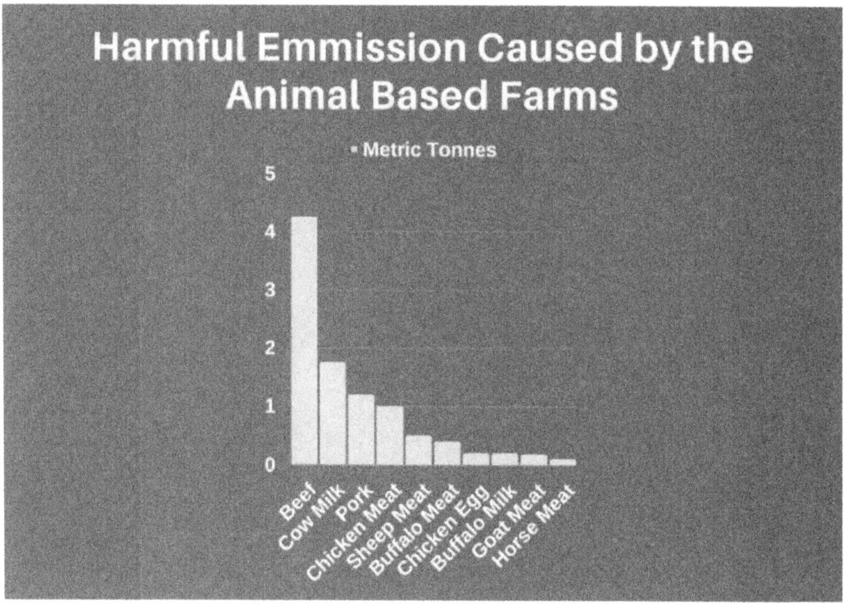

Benefits of veganism to the planet

Veganism has so many benefits for the planet and the environment. These benefits cannot be overlooked because they are enormous and will be listed below.

1. **Reduces overfishing**

Overfishing is a significant problem that faces water bodies in this age. Lots of the fishes are in danger of going extinct. Overfishing is detrimental to the aquatic ecosystem due to so many reasons. Overfishing is taking more fish out of the water than appropriate for balancing the water body and the specie. So many species of fish are extinct because of this behavior. The fishes that are not extinct are in danger of facing this fate. Many fishes, like some species of tuna and sharks, are hunted down for man's pleasure. They are hunted down to be eaten or kept in confinement which is very different from their natural habitat. The ones that are captured are subjected to inhumane conditions. Some of these fishes are made to reproduce as fast as possible, aiding them in being used commercially and as food. Even in confinement, these commercial houses bring wild fishes from the sea, which might introduce the spread of disease. Overfishing affects the aquatic body: reducing the number of fish, leading to the fast growth of seaweed, and competing with the remaining fish for oxygen. Being a vegan means you wouldn't eat fish, which means your lifestyle will decrease fish farming, which will cause a balance in the aquatic ecosystem.

2. **Prevents soil damage**

It might not add up when soil damage and livestock rearing are pitted under one-tenth. However, that is the reality of things. As more animals are reared on farms, their waste products are used to compensate and aid plant growth to provide more food for them. These waste products of these animals are not as mild as they seem; some have a strong chemical composition, which might aid the growth of the crop but eventually destroy it. Another potent soil destroyer is grazing. As the animal grazes on one land area for a long time, the soil loses strength. Also, more areas with trees and vegetation are destroyed to create more animal space. As the soil is left bare, added with the waste products of the animals, and grazing, swift destruction of soil ensues. As the soil is destroyed, it loses its strength and water-holding capacities, making it susceptible to further erosions, which is terrible for the environment. If not adequately handled, it can lead to landslides, and everyone knows the consequences. Being a vegan makes you want animals to stay in their natural habitat and not disturb the course of nature.

3. Reduces the release of greenhouse gases

Greenhouse gases are harmful carbon gases that are released into the atmosphere. If you have ever heard of chlorofluorocarbons (CFCs), a significant type of GHGs, you will understand the threat these gases pose to our atmosphere. These gases are so potent that they puncture the ozone layer when released into the atmosphere. The ozone layer, which protects us from the sun's harshness, loses its power. Hence, the world is beginning to experience global warming. The link between the GHGs and livestock rearing might not be discussed because people do not know the link between them. Methane which is a GHG, is released in gigatonnes to rear animals. Many processes in these animal factories need these gases to continue, like incubation and other extensive batch operation processes. Even though livestock farming is not the primary source of GHG emitted to the atmosphere, it contributes a substantial amount of GHG. This means being vegan will reduce the activities of these farm factories and lead to a saner environment and even climate.

4. Improves cleaner waterways

Naturally, clean water is a significant problem facing many countries today. Many opinions might beg to differ because they see a large blue water body altered by several chemicals to make it look clean. Naturally, clean water without aid from chemicals is hard to find today. Water is needed by every organism on this planet, not only fishes. As humans, we need water the most; even though we would not go to the wild to drink water, we might visit to swim well, and seeing the polluted river is a nasty sight. The primary source of water pollution from farming is livestock feed and antibiotics. These are used in rearing animals but can threaten fish's lives. As they are released into the water, they pollute the water and cause harm in two significant ways. The first way they do this is to kill some fish species when they are poured into the water. The second way they do this is by promoting an abnormal growth of sea algae which competes with the fishes for oxygen and eventually kills the fishes in the area. The second condition is known as the dead area. Being a vegan will decrease livestock farming, leading to a balance in aquatic life and cleaner water.

5. Reduces deforestation saves wildlife and endangered species

As the lands are cleared to accommodate the livestock needs and grow more food, it leads to deforestation. The land used to plant crops that feed animals was once forests and homes to wildlife. There are many detriments of deforestation that people ignore. Deforestation causes a release of carbon into the atmosphere. If the forests are left the way they are supposed to be, there will be no change in the gaseous exchange with the environment. These trees absorb the carbon dioxide for photosynthesis, giving us purer oxygen. If they are no longer there, there will be more carbon in the atmosphere than oxygen, which is detrimental to the cycle. The excess carbon in the atmosphere causes a change in water cycles, climates, and temperature.

Deforestation makes wildlife flee from their original habitat. Since the environment is no longer suitable or familiar to them, these animals flee from their homes to other places where they will be hunted and killed by hunters and poachers. As this continues, many species have become endangered. Deforestation has caused the extinction of many species, and if it continues, there will be an imbalance in the order of the planet. It will also lead to a restriction of movement in humans and animals because these areas will no longer be wildlife but considered private property. As a vegan, you will save the world from all the struggles; since you don't eat meat, deforestation will be reduced for livestock purposes.

Chapter 2
Why Is It So Hard?

Reading through all these, you might have become entranced with the idea of sticking with this new lifestyle. You must understand that just like every good thing in life comes the hard way, veganism is the same. It might be hard to practice veganism if you don't have the conviction or willpower to live by it. With the right inner strength, it might be hard to stand by it initially, but it will eventually be a smooth sailing ride.

The problem of lack of willpower

There are several reasons a person willing to begin veganism might lack willpower. However, not every reason might be experienced by every person since motivation is individual-specific. The following reasons listed below are the popular reasons why a person may shy away from pursuing veganism.

Causes of lack of willpower

1. Limited food choices

Most people grow up with an omnivorous diet and are accessible to plant and animal produce. When they think about beginning a vegan diet, the idea of limited food choices begins to weigh them down. It weighs them down and makes them halt between continuing with their former diets and starting the vegan diet. They have thoughts that becoming a vegan associate them with a limited type of food on the shelf when it is not so. Although a lot of food is available for people with omnivorous diets and other types of diets, the fraction available for vegans is smaller. Still, it should not be a thing that will cause demotivation. If you want to make food exciting with exciting colors, there are many vegan recipes. Although the constituents of the recipes are mostly the same; however, with different recipes, you can get entirely different food.

2. Financial problems

A key demotivator to beginning a vegan lifestyle is the price of vegan items. Although a person might not be poor, they would not want to spend all their money on food just because they want to change their diet. People consider things that will make them spend more than they intend useless for any pursuit. Others might beg to differ in this opinion, saying vegan foods are cheaper, but they honestly aren't. If a vegan spends their lives eating lentils, tofu, and other vegetables, they might save more money on food. However, that will make the lifestyle boring and without color. To add color to their meals, vegans might add lab-grown meat, salmon, and other alternatives to spice up their diet. Sometimes, they might add visiting a vegan restaurant at least thrice a month. All these are expenses. These things spice up the vegan lifestyle and are generally more expensive than animal products. The vegan industries receive less funding and subsidies for what they produce because there is a limited number of vegans worldwide; the products are more expensive. Going to a restaurant to purchase a burger, you will notice that the vegan burger is more expensive than the non-vegan burger because vegan meat is more expensive. So many other vegan products are more expensive than animal products. Due to this, many people interested in veganism might wait till they are more financially capable of affording these without breaking the bank. Even the ones with an average income, or a little higher than average, will find it hard to begin because of the priciness. However, if you wish to live a happy life, the priciness of a few vegan products should not hinder you from starting your vegan journey.

3. Fear of leaky gut

Since vegans do away with meat, fish, and other animal protein sources, which are popular, they resort to taking proteins from legumes and lentils. A diet where a person heavily depends on legumes and lentils is healthy but detrimental to the intestine. Since this book is not centered on the health aspects of veganism, more insights into the mechanism of action of the constituents of legumes on the intestine would not be written. Leaky gut is a condition where the intestine's permeability is increased, making it easy for an exchange between the toxic contents of the intestine and the bloodstream. Some people fear the occurrence of this, while others fear other gut-related problems like diarrhea. People believe that people who eat a plant-based diet are more prone to diarrhea than those who eat animal-based or omnivorous diets. This is a popular misconception about veganism that should be abolished. Veganism does not set anyone up for G.I. problems. There is no doubt that the stool of a vegan might be softer than that of a non-vegan, especially if they eat more fruits. However, apart from that, there is no proof that a vegan diet will cause diarrhea.

4. Fear of hormone disruption and other changes in body physiology

Some people might also be afraid of the consequences veganism might have on the hormone levels in a person. This fear is primarily for people who might have done extensive research on veganism and the effects some foods might have on the body's hormone release. This fear stems from the use of soy in making most vegan foods. Soy is used in making lab-grown meats, tofu, and vegan milk. Soy contains phytoestrogen, which promotes an increase in the release of estrogen. If the estrogen level in the body is increased, it will lead to an imbalance in the body's hormones. People are afraid of what this might do to them, forgetting that soy isn't the only thing that vegans eat. Vegans are open to other options which aren't soy. They can use almond and plant-based milk if they have enough soy milk.

Another change in physiology some people fear is a lack of hemoglobin; since veganism is an entirely plant-based diet, they believe it might not give the body the necessary elements required for hemoglobin production. Heme iron is needed by the body to produce hemoglobin, and heme iron is obtained solely from red meat. This is not a misconception; however, it is not entirely true. Other plant sources of iron can provide vegans with the iron their body needs to produce hemoglobin. Some supplements can make up for inadequate iron content in some plant sources. Although many people are not interested in supplements, if they don't want them, there are ways to balance their diets to ensure an adequate iron supply.

Some people also fear not getting an adequate amount of omega-3 fatty acid. As a vegan, a person will give up fish, and fish oil is the primary source of omega-3 fatty acids. Vegans do not take fish oil or anything made from fish. This fear might not entirely be wrong, but it is not entirely correct. This is because some supplements can stand in place of omega-3 fatty acids. So, omega-3 fatty acids should not stand in the way of your vegan lifestyle.

Vitamin B deficiency is another lack that makes people halt from beginning veganism. Most vitamin B12 are animal sources, making people skeptical about veganism. This should not be a hindrance; there are vitamin B12 supplements that can make up for the lack of this vitamin in a diet. There are so many trusted brands that produce these vitamins for those who have a vitamin deficiency diet.

Inhibition of zinc absorption is another fear that befalls people that want to begin veganism. Zinc is a micronutrient needed by the body for many functions. These people with this excuse might not know that there are many zinc plant sources, but their idea is not based on the availability of zinc in plant foods but on the absorption of zinc. Some plants have a pigment that might stop zinc absorption or slow it down. This reason should not be a reason that will make a person reconsider veganism because there are other sources of zinc if you decide not to get it from plants. There are zinc supplements that a physician can prescribe to replace the deficiency of zinc in foods.

5. Too much carbohydrate intake

Apart from vegetables and fruits, most of the foods available for vegans are regarded as carbohydrates. Grains and non-grain crops are primarily carbohydrates. Most people beginning a life of veganism believe that veganism will help them live healthier lives, so having a higher intake of carbohydrates than other nutrients can be counterproductive to this aim. The number of carbohydrates they will be exposed to as vegans make them question if they are making the right choice by choosing veganism. If you understand how meals work, this idea is just a temporary demotivator without power. Any diet can have a high intake of carbohydrates. A high carbohydrate intake, although common in veganism, is not uncommon among non-vegans. The fear of carbohydrates is because excess of it that is not used might be stored as fat and lead to obesity. Obesity makes a person susceptible to several diseases. Understanding how to mix your food as a vegan would not make you prey to a diet filled with carbohydrates. This might seem almost impossible since legumes, popularly considered a protein, contain more carbohydrates than protein. A mixture of beans and rice, which might have been considered a balanced meal of carbohydrates and protein, is more carbohydrate than protein. However, that should not hinder you from pursuing a vegan lifestyle. Other plant protein sources can be used alongside carbohydrate dishes. It goes down to how well you can balance your eating, not the number of carbohydrates available to you as a vegan.

6. Lack of energy to continue routine

In our busy world, there are many people with different routines. Some people have more tedious routines, while others have relaxed routines. Whatsoever the routine of a person might be, they need the energy to continue it effectively and meet their daily demands. This is also a reason why people reconsider veganism and the choices of foods. Since many people start with an omnivorous diet, they might feel it is more suitable to get the nutrients they need to function adequately during the day. However, that is not entirely true. Although a vegan diet excludes meat and dairy products, there is lots of energy packed in it. Carbohydrates are the principal source of energy that the body uses as fuel to function. Since there are different carbs available to vegans, having the energy to continue your daily routine is not a problem. A high carbohydrate vegan diet will require you to have an active day and expend the same energy you took in as food. So, suppose you are worried about having the energy to continue your daily routine after becoming a vegan. In that case, you should relieve yourself of that thought because, as a vegan, you will have lots of energy to continue living your everyday life and have more if you decide to pick up a hobby along with your routine.

7. Disordered eating probability

Many people are scared of veganism because of the similitude to extreme dieting. If there is a thing many people are skeptical about, it is extreme dieting. Undoubtedly, people have seen the effect of extreme dieting on people who became obsessed with the process. The obsession led to them living miserable lives. They begin to live as though they were in a cage, restricting their movements and monitoring every move they make. When people think about beginning veganism, they think of the strictness of the vegan diet and become afraid of the consequences of becoming one. They think of the probability of them developing an eating disorder. The most common eating disorder they become afraid of developing is orthorexia. This eating disorder is the obsession with eating healthy foods. A vegan diet is healthy and does not necessarily entail that you will become obsessed with a strict diet. Some fun vegan snacks are similar to non-vegan snacks. Although many people believe that vegans have orthorexia, it does not mean you cannot be a vegan without being obsessed with it. Veganism is not recruitment into an army; it can be taken at your pace.

8. Fear of social consequences of veganism

Another fear aspiring vegans have is the effect of veganism on their social life. Foods are served at several gatherings, friend, office, and acquaintance meetings. Foods bring many people together, and the fear of not eating what other people eat can hinder a person from becoming vegan. Going to a social event where a lot of snacks, foods, and drinks are available, but you can't eat or drink even though you are hungry because you're not sure of the ingredients used in preparation is frustrating. It might make you feel like veganism would try to separate you from your social circle. These people also consider the probability of their inability to discuss the taste of foods with friends and become the one picky friend in their circle. They consider what it would be like to avoid eating the meal that once bonded them to a person. They consider what it will be like to always get a different food from the general one served at the cafeteria. They consider the barrier it will bring them and their previous social life.

Another fear they might have was the prolonged time they spend grocery shopping or the idea of vegan products not readily available in the markets close to their home.

These fears are valid and solid demotivators but shouldn't be so. Living as a vegan does not mean you will b cut out from your social circle. Although you might not eat everything you used to before, with time, your friends and loved ones will get used to it and become more inclusive of you to ensure you partake in fun. You can always have a vegan snack bar in your pocket for public gatherings if watching people eat will make you hungry. You might not feel left out when you eat your snack bar while they eat. You can always bring your lunch pack with you for cafeterias at work or school to ensure you don't feel left out. It is even better to have your lunch pack because you will have the type of meal you love. For prolonged shopping time, there are vegan markets where you can quickly get these vegan foods to store till you need them. All these show that social constraints shouldn't be an option to stop you from living the vegan dream.

9. Fear of sustainability

As many people want to become vegan, a question that hovers over their minds is, "Is it sustainable?" many people have joined the vegan movement, but only a few were able to maintain it for months or years. Due to this, people believe that living a vegan lifestyle is hard and impossible to stand by. Starting a new thing is hard, but it is harder to keep up with it. Similarly, when people begin veganism with vigor, they believe they will be able to stay along with the lifestyle. However, motivation can only take you so far; sustainable habits make you last longer as a vegan. Not all vegans couldn't cope with the lifestyle; some people have been vegans for over twenty years, and it all boils down to individuality. Suppose you are determined and persistent in being a vegan, even though you practice it flexibly. In that case, you'll be able to sustain your lifestyle more than a person with initial motivation without continuous resolution. Fear of sustainability should not stop you from taking a step into veganism.

Consequences of lack of motivation

You might not see what lack of motivation is doing to you because you feel you should be able to start when you want to. The significant consequence of lack of motivation is achieving results later than expected. The moment you start the lifestyle, you start building yourself to receive the benefits on time, depending on why you chose the lifestyle.

If you choose veganism for health-related issues, then wasting time in to begin might be detrimental to you. Everything in life takes time to take effect and reach its finished product. Similarly, lifestyle change might take a while before a person starts reaping the rewards. This means that the more you delay the process, the farther you will be from the rewards.

Also, as you delay and keep up with animal eating, more animals will be killed, and the role you would have played in reducing the number of animals killed will no longer be there. The delay means you would be fighting with your conscience whenever you go to a fancy restaurant to eat a medium rare steak. Whenever you eat a delicious red chicken stew, you will also fight your conscience because you will think of the processes and pain the animal went through for its meat to be available to you. As you delay, you think of all the harsh factory processes the chickens had to go through to produce large eggs for you.

You will harm your conscience if you love burgers and continue eating them with the meat inside. It is a different ball game for people who have never been interested in veganism because they would have no concern when they eat these foods since they believe that they need these animal foods to survive.

However, as a person gaining interest in veganism, the previous ideologies you had concerning diets are gone, and the present mindset is solely geared towards protecting animals and eating a safe diet for you and the environment. There is a total change in your idea of diets. This means that the more you delay, the more you would have one more thing in your mind to bug you.

Why is it hard to hold on?

People on the verge of living vegan lifestyles consider it hard to hold on to. It is one of the sources of discouragement for those who want to become vegans. People would not want to start something they will get tired of quickly, so they might shy away from adopting the lifestyle. However, it is imperative to know that as many people began veganism but could not keep up with it, some people have maintained the lifestyle for several years. This means it is possible to stick to veganism if you have the willpower. Below are some reasons why a person might find it hard to continue the lifestyle.

1. The passiveness of attitude in the vegan lifestyle

A passive attitude toward the vegan lifestyle is a trait that shouldn't be found in any vegan looking to stick with veganism for life. A lack of motivation characterizes passiveness. A person not motivated to become a vegan does not see any critical reason why they should leave their previous lifestyle and embrace veganism. This type of person is aware of the benefits that veganism will bring to them and the environment. They know that veganism has many things to offer them, but they do not have the conviction about it. Due to the lack of motivation, this person will find it hard to change their attitude to fit in with this new lifestyle. There will be a similarity between their former and the present. Another sign of this passiveness is approaching veganism with a greedier and hungrier approach. They want to try everything and eat everything. They don't have the discipline to control their want for food. They believe in getting everything they want. This lifestyle stirs up negativity within them, which continues the demotivation process. They begin to have thoughts that tell them that the lifestyle is pointless or thoughts that tell them the lifestyle is punishment. As these negative thoughts build within, the person eventually falls out of veganism.

2. Choosing veganism only because of health reasons

Some people choose veganism because of health reasons. It is not wrong to become a vegan to improve some aspects of your health; however, that reason is not enough to keep you a vegan for a long time. This is what people fail to understand; hence, they brand veganism as a mere diet. Veganism is a lifestyle, and choosing a lifestyle solely because of health might not be enough to keep you in that lifestyle. No wonder people looking to lose weight choose veganism because of its effectiveness. However, they return to their previous lifestyle when they get their desired weight.

Similarly, people facing various health challenges might choose veganism if it will ease their pain and alleviate their illness. Like the weight loss group, they leave the lifestyle when they get relief. If you want to stick to veganism, you must not limit yourself to joining because of health reasons. Understand what living as a vegan is and the other reasons for veganism. When you understand all these, even though you get the result you are looking for, you will continue because you understand the benefits it brings to you.

3. Being with people who despise the vegan lifestyle

We might ignore the fact that people affect our lifestyle. People, we find ourselves in the midst of subconsciously shaping our thoughts and actions. No matter how resolute and firm your decisions are, what people say affects how you execute your thoughts. A person amid people who have vegans at the tip of their thoughts, whenever they want to make a bad reference, will find it challenging to stick with the lifestyle. This is not a step the person might take consciously, but without knowledge because we are in tune with our environment. A vegan with more vegans around them will find it easier to stick to the lifestyle than a vegan amid meat eaters. A vegan amid meat eaters might waver in their decision, especially if they are new to veganism. This situation is just like a person doing intermittent fasting in a room full of people eating their favorite snack. Although it might be possible for the person to continue with their intermittent fast, it is not if they are new to intermittent fasting. If you are strong enough to stay among meat eaters, that's okay but not recommended because it can take you back to your previous lifestyle. No matter the type of people you choose to surround yourself with, you should ensure they are not people who despise the vegan lifestyle. They should not be people that will discourage you from continuing being vegan because even though you don't believe their words, they will eventually come to your mind, making you ponder on the correctness of your choice. The longer time you spend pondering on your choice, the more likely it is for you to let go.

4. Being stuck on the previous lifestyle

Lots of people who start veganism do not detach themselves from their previous lifestyles before considering veganism. People stuck in their previous lifestyle will not move on and make the most out of the current lifestyle. Instead, they would spend their days brooding on the favorability of their life. This behavior will make it seem that veganism is a source of suffering for them. They might not profess that the lifestyle is rigorous, but their general outlook on the lifestyle will show that they are just dragging themselves about. It might show in ways like making reference to meat and its delicious taste, talking and thinking about the niceness of dairy and other animal products. A person who shows signs of being stuck in the past diet or missing the diet will find it hard to embrace veganism. Everything they do will remind them how much they miss the former way they ate. This behavior will lead to an abrupt switch back in the diet when they get the chance. If they try resilience, it will not be long before they return to their previous ways.

5. Choosing veganism for the wrong reasons

There are several purposes a person might choose veganism. Some might not be logical enough to sustain them as vegans. In an age where every celebrity is idolized, some people might choose to go vegan to 'twin' with their celebrity crush. It is okay to do things that connect you with a celebrity you adore; however, these things should not be brought to lifestyle. Choosing a type of lifestyle because a celebrity you know and love lives that way will make you confused about what your aims are. As you deprive yourself of meat because the celebrity you love hates it, you will be pitting yourself for a fall. The moment you stop loving that celebrity, there will be no driving force to continue. Even though you continue, it will be because you are dragging yourself. There will be no inner resolution and discipline to continue. The lifestyle becomes frustrating and depressing to keep up with as time goes by. A wrong reason is not only the influence of a celebrity; it could also be peer pressure or other trivial reasons. Beginning a vegan lifestyle requires you to think it through and consider your options if they suit you. A person who wants to begin veganism should have a personal conviction so that they will be sustained in practice.

6. Lack of thorough understanding of the lifestyle

There are ideas people have about veganism before they adopt the lifestyle. Some people look deeper to understand what it truly entails, while most rush into the lifestyle, basing their beliefs on some misconceptions they have heard in the media or from people who are not thoroughly versed on the topic. Due to this, they have so many misconceptions about veganism, which makes them pull out of the lifestyle after a few weeks or months of practicing. Some believe there is no difference between veganism and vegetarianism, which is an absolute lie. With a google search and little research, anyone can come in contact with the glaring differences. Some people do not also understand that there are strict vegans who don't wear any products from animals, and there are the flexible ones who occasionally wear them. These two types of people are similar but different in depth of practice. Not everyone is cut out to be a strict vegan; it is not a sustainable practice for people that will appreciate a little bit of flexibility. Suppose a person doesn't understand the differences between the two and believes that all vegans should practice strict veganism. In that case, they might put themselves in a straitjacket if they appreciate flexibility. Understanding the vegan lifestyle thoroughly makes you understand the options available and the one that is the most suitable for you to practice. If you practice veganism that suits you, you will enjoy your new lifestyle and sustain it for longer.

7. Creation of false reality

Some people create false realities for themselves once they become vegans. At the beginning stage of veganism, it is advised to keep a vegan company that will aid you in sustaining your lifestyle. This is a piece of very accurate advice that grounds you in your vegan journey. However, it can become detrimental to your lifestyle when it is on the extreme. A person who surrounds themselves with only vegans becomes caught up in a vegan bubble. This vegan bubble comprises vegan ideas, people, and virtually everything vegan. A person living in this bubble becomes desensitized to the non-vegan diet, people, and lifestyle. This might seem like a good thing, but it is not. As a person living in the world, you must be informed about every aspect. Limiting yourself to that vegan bubble will cause a social barrier between you and non-vegans, which is unnecessary since there is no guarantee you will always be with vegans for the rest of your life. As this type of person is aware of only vegans, they begin to believe that many people in the world are vegans and lose touch with reality. They forget that only a few of the world's population are vegans. When you lose touch with the reality of your lifestyle, you begin to lose purpose and discipline for your course. Loss of focus, purpose, and discipline will lead to returning to the lifestyle.

Chapter 3
The Enemy Of My Enemy Is My Friend

The people around us affect the decisions we make and the lifestyles we keep up with. As social beings, the behavior and ideas of people around us tend to affect us positively or negatively. If we overlook the kind of company we keep and the outlook of their company on our lifestyle, we might get confused when things do not go as planned.

External stimuli

External stimuli are the external factors and their influence on a person. A thing to be a stimulus has to affect a person. Several sources of external stimuli, some notable ones that play essential roles in people's lives, are family members, friends, acquaintances in the same social circle, colleagues, the environment, and the media.

Family members

Family members are a stimulus source, especially if the family is always close. A person with a close-knit family will receive more stimulation from family than other people. The type of family they have will affect their choice of clothes, food, and lifestyle in general. Family members' influence on a person might not be entirely planned or forced. However, that doesn't mean that all their influence is subconscious and non-vocal; some of these influences come from how they reason about situations shown in their words and actions. As time goes on, their thoughts merge with those of family members. These thoughts are not always negative; sometimes, it is positive; the bottom line suggests that the thought and behavior of the person are affected by the influence of the family members.

Friends

Friends are an excellent stimuli source. When people think of friends as influencing a person, they consider peer pressure. Peer pressure might be one of the influences friends have on other friends, but it is only a minute compared to the subconscious influence they have on a person. These people might not dictate how they want their friends to live because they have no right to. However, when they comment on a subject or show their ideas about a subject using their actions, the brain subconsciously registers their view. As more input is made on that subject, it subconsciously shapes the person's mind concerning that matter. The person subconsciously shapes their behavior to fit in with the idea of their friends. It might seem that the person is copying their friends, but they are not. They are tuning themselves to the stimuli from their friends. They begin to see their lifestyles change from the ones their friends have. The change is constant but without their notice. Sometimes, they never notice that their friends influence them until they consider changing some habits.

Acquaintances in social circle

As humans, we tend to behave to get people to like us, especially people we hold in high esteem. So, the idea these people will have about us shapes our behavior. This is not a conscious act; it is unconscious. As we often hang out with these people, we subconsciously want to fit into the circle in every area. The things they say, their opinions about matters shape your ideas. The way they behave determines the firmness of your lifestyle and flexibility. People in your social circle don't have to be friends with you; they can just be people you know and talk to often. Just like friends, their ideas are engraved into you subconsciously and consciously. Their views about some matters might allow you to view different things from perspectives different from yours. Even though you are opinionated and steadfast in your decisions, you might waver in your perspectives because there will be other perspectives to consider.

Colleagues

These are the least expected people to affect our lives, but they play a substantial role. If you go to work every day, it is least likely for you not to interact with at least one of your colleagues. Even though you are a loner that doesn't like interacting with people, there will be times you will need to interact for business reasons. Interaction with people means there will be an exchange of ideas and notions verbally. As we have conversations with people, it registers in our minds even after the conversation is over. These conversations can affect a person without their knowledge. If you go to work and the person you are the closest to constantly criticizes the pronunciation of the letter' A,' you will subconsciously start thinking ill about the pronunciation of that letter that never bugged you, and you never took cognizance of it. This is why some kids come back home and behave a certain way because their classmates say something about it. If the influence from colleagues is constant, it might alter the previous lifestyle of a person. Although colleagues might affect a person's behavior, they have a low influence compared to family, friends, and social circle.

Environment

The environment or area we live in also influences our choices and lifestyles. The environment can be considered a major mental stimulant. Many people change according to the environment they move to. It is not like the saying that you have to behave like a roman in Rome because of an unconscious move done by the brain to fit into that environment. No wonder a person will behave a certain way in a country and change lifestyle when they move. We tend to be affected by the things we see around us. If a person moves to a place that believes wearing a jacket in the summer is incredible, they might join in the notion. They might not enjoy following trends or understanding the notion, but they will because they would not want to be excluded from anything that was done – they want to fit in perfectly. The environment also plays an imperative role in our lifestyles and eating. If a more significant percentage of people living in an environment likes a particular thing, that thing will be more available in stores. Thus, its availability will shape the lifestyle of the people in that environment. People who don't like using it will eventually try to make themselves use it because it is available more than they want. If they cannot cope by making themselves like what they hate, they might change environments or become stressed because what they want is not available. The environment is a broad term for all the stimuli a person can get from their environment. The stimuli can be people, animals, ideas, food, and any other thing in the environment that stimulates the mind.

Social media

If it was in the 19th or 20th century, social media might not be mentioned as a factor that is a source of external stimuli. With the rise of social media in the 21st century, more people are engrossed in it than in their physical environment. Social media affects people just like the environment does. People watch videos on social media and interact with strangers, but they unknowingly imbibe some cultures. For example, most people hear about veganism for the first time on social media or T.V. Before they heard of it, they never knew that such a movement existed, probably because no one around them practiced this lifestyle. As humans, we are more stimulated by what we see. This means that as we handle our phones to watch videos on the internet, these videos are stored in some part of our mind, gradually shaping how we see things. The first reaction to watching a video where a leech attacks a woman on her first day at work at a reserve will be fear. This fear might not be recognized until you are taken to a similar-looking reserve and afraid to enter. Things we hear on media, like T.V. and radio, affect our lifestyle and choices. Gradually, our lives begin to take a turn that will fit into what we see and admire in the media.

Types of stimuli

Two major types of stimuli can shape your lifestyle and choices. These stimuli are opposites and peculiar depending on the factors caused.

1. Positive stimuli
2. Negative stimuli

Positive stimuli

This type of stimuli is the type that gets a positive reaction out of us. A positive stimulus can be a good friend that changes our lifestyles for the better. It can also be a positive stimulus when you interact with people at work positively, and the interaction yields positive stimulation in your mind. Generally, positive stimuli help us focus on our worthy goals and make us happier and more in tune with a good lifestyle. A positive stimulus will encourage a person to live a good lifestyle. Summarily, positive stimuli make people grow and enhance their motivation to do good.

Negative stimuli

A negative stimulus gets an adverse reaction from us. A word or action is not a negative stimulus only when it makes us react with anger. There are various emotions a person might react with if they are stimulated negatively. Some people might not react, but it will affect their lifestyles without their knowledge. These negative stimuli work in the area of demotivation. Their sole aim is to discourage a person from their lifestyle. Negative stimuli's effect is different depending on the source of stimulation. For example, a person who has a healthy lifestyle void of cigarettes might be tempted to know what it feels like if they stay in an environment that encourages smoking to chase chilly feelings. The stimuli from the people might be unintentional and come in several ways. It might be in ways where they glorify their habits of smoking or in ways where they make healthy habits seem like a waste of time since everyone will eventually die, and none of those will matter afterward. These are ways they might discourage a person. New vegans might be affected by negative stimuli if they are not surrounded by like-minded people or people who tolerate other people with lifestyles that are different. The people around you determine how firm and enjoyable your vegan journey will be. Positivity or negativity through the vegan journey depends on external feedback from people and the environment.

Effects of negative external stimuli on veganism

There are many consequences that negative stimuli from those around you can cause to your vegan journey. You can ignore these consequences, but it is essential not to if you want to live a sustainable vegan life. If you consider where you would have been if you didn't make those poor choices because of the influence of other people on your life, you will notice that people's feedback plays a role in how your life is, then you may realize. There are lots of effects that negative stimuli might have on your vegan journey. However, there are three main ways it might do this.

- **Make veganism unsustainable for you**

Anybody that wants to become a vegan for the right reasons would not want to become a vegan today and lose interest in it tomorrow. Since ethical reasons are one of the right reasons, a person will prefer saving animals till the day they die than saving animals for a while before going back to eat them. This sustainability is only achieved by people who are surrounded by positive energy. A person with negativity will practice veganism with thoughts of giving up because of external discouragements. They get tired because people around them do not understand their lifestyle; there is no compromise by these people to make them feel included. There are no vegan snacks bought to make them included. This kind of person might not be surrounded by people who outrightly say veganism is terrible, but these people's actions suggest that they think it is not worth it. It might not seem to matter when they are insensitive initially, but eventually, it starts registering in the mind and the behavior. It leads to the person rethinking their decision before eventually abandoning the lifestyle in search of greener pastures.

- **Make you contemplate your decision**

Negative feedback from friends who are non-vegans can affect your faith in veganism. To practice veganism to the fullest, you have to believe in the correctness of your choice and how it is positively affecting you and the planet. If you lose this confidence in your decision and begin to contemplate, you will lose the motivation to continue as a vegan. The loss of motivation does not come once to make you leave veganism. It is a gradual process where painful thoughts cloud your mind. You might begin to have thoughts like,

"Is this lifestyle worth it? What's my gain?"

"How will just my practice affect the world?"

"Life is short, and I'd spend it eating bland herbivore meals?"

"Do I need to do this?"

"Isn't it a bit impractical to give up dairy?"

"Is the increase in food expenses worth it? "

These are some things you will consider when contemplating your decision. Contemplating your decision will not be helpful; it will only help you drag yourself around veganism. You'd become like a person without purpose who does not understand why they are doing their routine but believe it's essential for them too.

- **Make veganism more stressful than enjoyable**

Veganism is a lifestyle, and a lifestyle can be chosen. The aim of having a lifestyle is to live in a way that you get the most out of life, which brings you happiness and peace. If people who stimulate you negatively are around you, you will notice that instead of enjoying and being happy with your vegan lifestyle, you become tired, stressed, and afraid of telling people about it. Some of these people make you afraid of being a vegan because how they tease you for being righteous in your own eyes because you spare animals from suffering. They say that not because they hate you but because that is what they think you are a vegan for. It makes it tougher to live life when you are always meticulous about what you do and say so you don't provoke negative talks. Some might not make it seem like you're pretending to be good but will argue with you the slightest chance they get. Since they don't understand veganism, they would bring up their ideas about why they think veganism isn't logical. Spending minutes and hours arguing your stance will leave you tired and stressed.

Chapter 4
What If I Told You There Is A Solution?

The abrupt change model is problematic and has a lot of loopholes that make it ineffective for a new vegan. There is a way you can practice veganism without being threatened by losing willpower along the way. Loss of willpower is one of the consequences of the incorrect practice of veganism. It might seem normal and doesn't cause much to your vegan life. However, it is not so; losing willpower can change your life into a more discouraging one. The previous chapter covered most of the consequences of losing motivation as a new vegan.

Some people might have tried to begin veganism many times but failed, not knowing their problem was a lack of willpower. Some signs can help you tell when you lack will.

Six main signs show the lack of willpower experienced by a person that's a new vegan or aspiring to become one.

1. Easy overwhelmed feeling:

Feeling overwhelmed by the lifestyle is one of the feelings that people that lack willpower experience. They might not show that they feel overwhelmed; it is more of a personal feeling.

A person feeling overwhelmed about veganism after beginning will spend their days and nights thinking about how their lifestyle will be in years to come. This feeling inside them is joined with a hint of fear that drives them into a crazy loop of thoughts.

This is quite different from feeling considering one's decision. It comes like an intrusive thought, and all the emotions attached to thinking about the future are added to the exhaustion. The idea of how it would make them already feel exhausted, and they have to pretend to like being vegan.

2. Lack of goal orientation:

Usually, when people choose the lifestyle they want, they choose a goal they want to achieve during those years. Some people who prefer a lifestyle attached to healthy eating might have plans to lose weight, maybe twenty kilograms, within a year. Others might choose a goal to save a hundred dollars in a year. Some others might have goals to clear their debts within a year.

The bottom line of choosing a lifestyle has a goal you would want to achieve. If no plan is attached, you lack the willpower to continue your lifestyle or have even fully lived in that lifestyle.

A vegan without a goal is as good as not being a vegan. There is no motivated vegan that would say they have no reason they are vegan. There is no vegan without an aim that they are looking forward to.

One vegan's aim might be to become a vegan to feel healthier and lighter, while another vegan's purpose might be because of their religion or belief. Some vegans might choose veganism for ethical reasons and their desire to preserve the environment.

No vegan is a vegan without reason. The desire to achieve their motives is the driving force that will help a person to achieve their aim. If there is no reason why you are vegan, then you will be de-motivated. It is just like a person that wakes up and does not know where they are. If you notice that you don't know your goals for being vegan, you have to go back to your drawing board because it will make you lose your willpower. If you lose willpower, you will not be happy as a vegan.

3. Confusion about what you want:

A significant sign of loss of motivation is confusion about what you want. Usually, when you have an aim, you would like to achieve it. Amongst all your purposes, a sole objective always makes you live the way you do.

Similarly, in veganism, there are things people want because, for this reason, they put their all into veganism.

Some people might want to create a safer place for animals, so they choose veganism. Some other people might choose veganism because they want to create a cleaner environment. These people that want to create a cleaner environment might choose veganism because it reduces the number of carbon emissions that comes from meat processing and other animal product processing. They might also decide on veganism so fewer animals will be reared, leading to deforestation and dirtier waterways. Whichever way they go about their veganism, the bottom line is that they want to create a cleaner environment for the planet.

A person might want many other things that will make them choose veganism.

If you have nothing you want from veganism, don't you think it's strange?

This means you don't know why you are practicing it, which is sad.

Even though you are pushing yourself around your practice to make sure you stick to your veganism, it does not mean you will be able to hold on for long.

Wanting something pushes you to be better and strive to stay on track. It is a type of internal motivation that no one can give you. If you notice that you don't know what you want from veganism anymore, it should be a sign that you lack the will to continue.

4. Losing control of your physical health:

Willpower is an essential factor that keeps our physical health in check. For a person to lose control of their physical health, especially weight, they lack the willpower to manage it adequately as it should.

Similarly, vegans without willpower will notice that they cannot keep their physical health in check.

Mostly, people say vegans have the highest rate of improved physical health. Although this is true, it does not apply to all the vegan population. Some vegans have no desire to practice veganism to the fullest and think believing the statistics will make them part of the statistics.

Even though people say vegan food is much healthier than others, you can still eat unhealthily as a vegan. Since many carbohydrates are available for vegan meals, it is easier for people to eat above their dietary needs if they aren't careful enough.

If you have the willpower as a vegan, you can inquire and search for meals and their dietary contents to keep your health in check. Being a vegan would not save collapsing physical health, but it can make your health much better if you practice it adequately.

5. You procrastinate most of the time:

People who lack willpower never get things done; they procrastinate until they forget that they have to do something.

Similarly, vegans or aspiring vegans who lack willpower will always procrastinate. If they are flexible vegans that want to become full vegans, they will procrastinate taking the step into full veganism.

Their procrastination might go on for years. This procrastination is not only limited to flexible vegans but aspiring vegans. Many people desire to become vegans, but because of several reasons that aren't important, they are afraid of taking a step.

These people might make thousands of inquiries about everything veganism. They might decide that this lifestyle is the best for them. Still, they would halt before taking the first step required to change their lifestyle. They might give excuses as to why they still haven't begun, but they could if they have the willpower.

Since lack of willpower stems from several reasons, there are several reasons why a person might procrastinate. Despite what reason it might be, taking the first step is an essential task for you to live the life you want.

6. You feel lost:

Most people who have lost the willpower to continue in a habit or lifestyle begin to feel lost most of the time. Feeling lost has a lot of feelings attached.

Sometimes, it might come from feeling overwhelmed because you don't recognize your lifestyle anymore. You begin reconsidering your decisions and their correctness, which might affect how you feel and your emotional reaction towards them. You don't know how to react to how they think; they don't know if what is right or their direction is right.

Vegans also feel lost when they feel that their veganism is going out of their control, and they don't understand if they should be vegan or switch back to their previous diet.

These vegans do not understand why they should eat plant-based diets anymore. They start considering if they are causing harm by drinking milk that doesn't hurt the animal. Their thoughts are full of conflict, and they cannot see why they continue with the same lifestyle when tired. Feeling this way will eventually lead to them leaving veganism, but a significant sign of lack of willpower.

Negative external stimuli are an essential factor that cannot be overemphasized.

We are greatly affected by the people we have around us and the kind of things they say to us. Even though we ignore the words they say and rule them out as having an impact on us, this happens all the time without us knowing. If we continue being exposed to harmful stimuli from people around us, we will not succeed in our vegan journey. Don't just ignore the negativity that comes from people; stay away from the negativity. Negativity is contagious, and before you know it, you will start thinking along the same lines, leading to losing focus on your goal when you choose veganism.

When you don't achieve your goal when you become a vegan, it may make you lose your self-esteem. Both negative stimuli from people and unachieved goals can cause low self-esteem.

Many people with low self-esteem do not know that they have low self-esteem because they do not introspect and think these other people have more worth than them.

Low self-esteem in a vegan stems from these factors might show in several ways. However, a few of the common patterns will be tackled.

- **Harsh self-criticism**

It might be a sign of low self-esteem if you constantly rebuke yourself whenever you fall short of your expectations. Harsh self-criticism is more than we think; it involves a series of self-demeaning thoughts that invade the mind.

During self-criticism, you might see yourself repeating some words you remembered from your negative external stimuli.

If you eat an omnivore meal after becoming a vegan just because you couldn't hold back for too long, you find yourself saying mean things like you are an enemy. You continue this way, probably to spur yourself to do better but end up feeling like you aren't worth anything but a massive failure in anything you do.

- **Ignoring achievements as a vegan and focusing on the setbacks.**

Some people might find it hard to embrace a fully vegan lifestyle, but because of their love for nature and animals, they might strive to be vegan. A little thing as much as a person going vegan for a week should be a thing they should celebrate. The celebration does not mean that the person has to rent a venue and invite guests to tell them that they have achieved a lot by sticking to their vegan meal for a week. If a person does that, it will be completely absurd. You don't also need to go to social media to blow your trumpet of making it to one week without eating as an omnivore.

Most times, saying the little wins out is because we don't believe they are wins, so we want people's validation to make us feel good for getting it.

Celebrating your win could be just returning your thoughts before you start and how far you've gone. You could also treat yourself as a way of celebrating that win; that way, you make yourself feel good. Telling loved ones about it is also a way of celebrating.

A person with low self-esteem would never celebrate or acknowledge their little or big wins in their vegan journey. Instead, they would capitalize on their shortcomings. No matter how little the drawback is, they would rather brood over it for weeks than focus on the headway they make on their vegan journey.

- **Thinking other people practice it better than you**

You hear people say, "I am not even vegan enough."

This mentality is a mentality of a person with low self-esteem caused by negative external stimuli. No matter how strict they are about their vegan practice, they still don't believe they are suitable vegans. Sometimes they even call themselves dirty vegans.

Everyone practices a lifestyle in the way that suits them most, not in the way that will conform to the pattern of another's routine. If you move from thinking this way to thinking that you have to practice your veganism the way a person is practicing theirs, you have moved away from the point you are supposed to be.

It would be better to look at some well-practicing vegans to understand what veganism entails. However, it does not mean you must copy the person's lifestyle in totality and brand yourself a failure when you don't practice.

The imperative thing is that you are practicing veganism and contributing to the safety of animals and the environment. The other things do not matter, so don't bother. If you notice that you think this way, You might need to get rid of the negative stimuli around you that are causing you to lose your self-esteem.

- **Unable to handle criticisms**

People who don't know how to handle criticisms criticize themselves, so hearing from another person might make them lash out emotionally. Similarly, people already fighting internal battles with themselves and their veganism might find it hard to take criticisms regarding veganism.

Criticisms are important sometimes to keep us in check. Some seem to like it out of maliciousness, but some have fundamental elements. It is essential to consider them before you discard them.

Inability to take criticism might be a sign that you have been stimulated negatively continuously and have developed low self-esteem over time. This should be a sign that you should remove yourself from any situation that will make you stimulated negatively.

- **Fear of failing**

Fear of failure is a significant sign of low self-esteem. You will always be afraid of failing if you have low self-esteem from negative stimulation.

Vegans with low self-esteem no longer believe in themselves and are always afraid to return to their previous lifestyle. They are scared of being tempted to give up on their veganism. Their fear becomes like a prison that they do not try other vegan-omnivore alternatives that could make veganism fun.

They try to stay in a one-patterned lifestyle so they don't mistakenly go astray. Failure happens sometimes, and it is not something that should be dreaded like a snake. If you fail in one day, you can always pick yourself up and start from where you stopped.

A life free from vegan-failure fear is a vegan life full of fun and lived to the fullest. If you have this attitude towards your lifestyle, you should do away with the source of fear so that your vegan life can be happier.

All these factors that come with low self-esteem can be avoided if the appropriate approach to veganism is taken.

There is an alternative way to become vegan without following this strict approach. If there were no other way to approach veganism, there would probably be fewer vegans than there are today. In every situation, there is always an easy way out.

It would be best if you did not give up on veganism because you cannot fit into the typical approach. It is okay not to be able to fit into the ordinary things people do; everyone is different and has something that will work for them.

So, if you are a new vegan, do not be afraid there is a way that you can practice veganism without experiencing all the emotional turmoil you've already gone through. If you are an aspiring vegan, there is a fun way to approach veganism that will have you smiling and happy to practice veganism for many years.

Chapter 5

Individuals And Populations, Statistics, And Large Numbers

"Understand the choice of veganism works better if it doesn't only apply to individuals but populations."

This statement might be hard to understand since it is known that everyone cannot practice veganism at the same time, and the vegan population is not as large as the media portrays it. This statement means that to understand your choice as a vegan, you must understand its application to people and not just individuals. You have to know how your lifestyle as a vegan will affect the population compared to an omnivore diet.

Every diet has a positive or a negative impact on the animal population. If you compare these variables, you will understand if your choice is worth it for you to continue or if it will be better for you to make another choice. However, through this, you will understand how correct your preference is and the animals you're saving from suffering with the approximate statistical analysis.

Average Omnivorous Meal (AOM)

Non-vegan foods create animal suffering, and this animal suffering created by a non-vegan diet can be quantified and measured by **Average Omnivorous Meal (AOM).** An average omnivorous meal is a variable used to represent the minimum unit of animal suffering a person creates by eating a diet partially or entirely made up of animal produce. This means that even if the product is not meat, but from animals, it causes a unit of suffering. As the animal product is derived, manufactured, modified, and acquired from sellers, it generates animal suffering that is represented in each meal as One unit.

To understand this better, you must consider your daily meals and how omnivorous they are. Remember, one purely omnivorous meal equals one (1) unit of animal suffering. If you eat three (3) omnivorous meals daily, you have generated three (3) units of animal suffering. If this continues for a month, you will cause more animal suffering.

One month = 30 - 31 days

Average unit of animal suffering per day = 3 (from three pure omnivorous meals.)

Average number of sufferings in a month = (30 x 3) - (31 x 3)

The average number of animals suffering in a month = 90 - 93 units.

That means eating omnivorous diets for one month will, on average, cause animals to suffer by a minimum of 90 units. This excludes the omnivore snacks that might be had in between meals of the day, especially at lunch hour. It also excludes the desserts you might have during the month.

To understand better, we will calculate it using a meal table that indicates the type of meal and snacks in a day.

Days	Breakfast	Lunch	Dinner	No. of omnivorous snacks in a day
Sunday	O.M. diet	O.M. diet	O.M. diet	3
Monday	OM diet	O.M. diet	O.M. diet	1
Tuesday	O.M. diet	O.M. diet	O.M. diet	0
Wednesday	O.M. diet	O.M. diet	O.M. diet	2
Thursday	O.M. diet	O.M. diet	O.M. diet	0
Friday	OM diet	O.M. diet	O.M. diet	3
Saturday	O.M. diet	O.M. diet	O.M. diet	5

O.M. means omnivorous diet. This table represents the type of diet eaten by a person throughout a month. One unit of animal suffering is not only expressed in full meals or cooked foods; it also includes snacks and desserts. The word snacks are used to refer to snacks, desserts, and appetizers that are derived from animal products.

If we calculate this like this, it is clear that the average number of animal suffering caused in a day will be greater than three because of the snacks eaten between meals.

On Sunday, one omnivorous meal was eaten in the morning for breakfast, another for lunch and dinner, making it a total of three omnivorous meals during the day. Since most people don't work on Sunday, Sunday might be a day they set for relaxation. During relaxation, they might eat more snacks than average. According to the table, this person eats three omnivorous snacks on Sundays.

Sunday= 1 + 1 +1 + 3 = 6

After adding all the omnivorous meals, including snacks, six omnivore meals were discovered.

The unit of animal suffering caused by this person on Sunday = 6 x 1 = 6

This means that this person caused six units of animal suffering on Sunday.

Similarly, suppose the unit of animal suffering caused by this person on Monday is considered. In that case, the person eats three omnivorous meals on Monday and one omnivorous snack for a lunch break. This means that this person ate four omnivorous meals on Monday. Eating four meals on Monday means the person caused four units of suffering.

On Tuesday, no omnivorous snack was eaten during the day, but three omnivorous meals were eaten breakfast, lunch, and dinner. This means that the number of suffering caused to animals was lower compared to other days. The unit of suffering caused to animals on Tuesdays are three units.

This person went on to have two omnivorous snacks on Wednesday, which equals two units of animal suffering. Furthermore, they had three omnivorous meals breakfast, lunch, and dinner. If all the omnivorous meals are added, it will be five omnivorous meals consumed on Wednesday. Consuming five omnivorous meals equals causing five units of animal suffering.

Just like Tuesday, on Thursday, this person does not eat snacks but eats three omnivorous meals, which equals three units of animal suffering caused in the day.

For most, Friday, the last day of the working week, is also a day for relaxation, which might make people lean more towards snacks. This person eats three snacks on Friday, equal to three units of suffering caused to animals. The person also eats three omnivorous meals, equivalent to three animal suffering units. If the units of animals suffering in a day are totaled, it would equal six units of animal suffering.

Saturday seems like the laziest day of the week because the break from the hustle and bustle of the week is the day many consume snacks more than usual. This person consumes five omnivorous snacks equal to five units of suffering. Since the person has a highly omnivorous diet, the three main courses are omnivorous.

5 (from snacks) + 3 (from breakfast, lunch and dinner) = 8

Therefore, this person causes eight units of animal suffering on Saturdays.

There are thirty to thirty-one days in a month, which means the number of times this person causes animal suffering is not in the tens.

Suppose there are five Mondays, Tuesdays, and Wednesdays in that month, with four other days. The days with five will be multiplied by five and four similarly.

There are four Sundays in that month

Sundays = 6 (units of suffering) x 4 (No. of Sundays in the month) = 24 units of suffering

There are five Mondays to Wednesday

Monday = 4 (units of suffering) x 5 (No. of Sundays in the month) = 20 units of suffering

Tuesday = 3 (units of suffering) x 5 (No. of Sundays in the month) = 15 units of suffering

Wednesday = 5 (units of suffering) x 5 (No. of Sundays in the month) = 25 units of suffering

There are four Thursdays to Saturdays

Thursday = 3 (units of suffering) x 4 (No. of Sundays in the month) = 12 units of suffering

Friday = 6(units of suffering) x 4 (No. of Sundays in the month) = 24 units of suffering

Saturday = 8 (units of suffering) x 4 (No. of Sundays in the month) = 32 units of suffering

If the total animal suffering in a month is calculated by adding the units of suffering from each day, what will be the real suffering in a month?

Total animal suffering caused in a month = 24 + 20 + 15 + 25 + 12 + 24 + 32 = 152 units of suffering.

This means this person caused 152 units of suffering in a month, unassisted! Think of how high the numbers will go each month. If this person continues with this lifestyle for one year, the number of animals suffering will be more massive than this.

One year = 12 months.

Animal suffering caused in a year = 1824

If this person continues this lifestyle for five years, animal suffering will increase.

Animal suffering caused in five years = 1824 x 5 = 9120 units.

This means one person can cause almost 10,000 units of animal suffering in five years.

This person used as a critical study might be someone who believes in minimalism and tries not to stuff their face in food. In another case, a person might eat more than this person, and the average units of suffering may get up to 10,000, or in some cases, more.

Population statistics

Remember that vegans are among the minority of the dietary population in the world. There are many more omnivores than vegans in the world. This means more families are omnivores than families that are vegans. It is not a thing that should be surprising since lots of people grow up with omnivorous diets, even some vegans. A family with omnivores will increase the unit of animal suffering: the more the omnivores, the more animal suffering increases.

Suppose a family comprises seven omnivores who eat omnivorous snacks at different rates. The amount of animal suffering caused by them in a year will be 1824 multiplied by seven.

The average unit of animal suffering caused by an omnivorous family of seven will be 12,768. This unit of suffering depends on how much they either maintain their intake of an omnivore diet. If they decide to increase their omnivore diet, maybe throw meat and eggs in as side dishes, the unit of suffering they will cause to animals collectively might be up to 13,000 units a year or more.

If they have had a similar diet for five years, the animal suffering they cause to animals during that period may increase to 63,840 units if their omnivore diet can grow as much as 65,000 or more. If they reduce their omnivore diet, it can go as low as 60,000 units. However, this is still not enough to stop animal suffering.

The population's suffering unit should be considered to understand the role of veganism in preventing animal suffering.

To understand this better, we would use a table of communities that shows the percentage of vegans.

Name of Community	Percentage of non-vegans	Percentage of vegans	Town's population
Town A	90	10	680
Town Q	50	50	730
Town B	10	90	367
Town E	100	0	926

Since this population is more generalized, the total number of suffering caused by one individual in one month will be 93. It is given as 93 because it cannot be generalized that every person in the community eats omnivore snacks alongside meals. The number 93 is arrived at after calculating the three meals eaten multiplied by the days in a month.

If we consider Town A, which has 90 percent non-vegans, and 10 percent non-vegans, we notice that the vegans are on the declining percentile.

Town's population = 680

Vegan percentage = 10

Non-vegan population = 90

Number of people who are vegans = 10% of 680 = 68 people

Number of people who are non-vegans = 680 – 68 = 612 people.

Average monthly unit of animal suffering to animals in Town A = 612 x 93 = 56,916.

If everyone were an omnivore in the town, the unit of suffering that animals would have received would have been 63,240. This analysis shows that although the vegans in town A are not up to a hundred, their role in alleviating animal suffering is substantial, although others might not be known. If the omnivores continue for five years, they will cause 284,580 units of animal suffering. The vegans in that community reduced the units of animals suffering by 6,324, which is quite impressive for an impact done by only sixty-eight people. If the vegans continue for five years, they will reduce animal suffering by 31,620.

If we consider Town Q, the next on the table, we would see an equal percentage of vegans and non-vegans in that community.

Town's population = 730

Percent of vegans in the town = 50

Percent of non-vegans in the town = 50

Number of people who are vegans = 50% of 730 = 365

Number of people who are non-vegans = 730 – 365 = 365

Average monthly unit of animal suffering to animals in Town Q = 365 x 93 = 33,945 units

If every 730 people had an omnivore dietary pattern, then the number of suffering animals received in a month would be 67,890. Thankfully, half of the population is vegan, so the unit of animal suffering became half of what it would have been. The vegans reduced the average animal suffering by 33,945 units, lower than town A, which has a lower population. If people with an omnivorous diet continue for five years, they will cause 169,725 units of animal suffering. Meanwhile, vegans will save animals from suffering with the same unit.

Town B seems like a small settlement of vegans because the population comprises ninety percent and ten percent non-vegans. In this population, there is a decline of omnivores and a predominance of vegans.

Town's population = 367

Vegan percentage = 90

Non-vegan population = 10

Number of people who are vegans = 90% of 367 = 330 people

Number of people who are non-vegans = 367 – 330 = 37 people.

Average monthly unit of animal suffering to animals in Town B = 3,441 units

If every person in this town were an omnivore, the unit of animal suffering would have been 34,131. However, since most of the populace are vegans, the number of animals suffering was reduced by 30,690. If the vegans continue that way for five years, they will reduce animal suffering by 153,450. Even if the omnivores in this town continue for five years, it will be 17,205 units of suffering, which is considerably low compared to the impact of veganism.

In Town E, it is clear that there are no vegans in the population of 926 people. This means that the units of animals suffering caused by this town will be greater than in the other cities.

Everyone in town E is an omnivore, which means there will be no reduction in animal suffering in the presence of vegans.

The average monthly unit of animal suffering caused by Town E = 926 x 93 = 86,118 units.

This means that Town E contributes 86,118 units to animal suffering every month. Since there is no vegan in that town, there is no one to subsidize the units of suffering caused. If this continues for five years, 430,590 units of suffering will be impacted. The numbers will only go up if there is no change in the coming years.

From these, you can deduce that if a person isn't wholly vegan but try eating as a vegan, they would impact the units of animal suffering caused by month and year.

Chapter 6

How The Common Approach Works And Why It Doesn't Work

You can choose the traditional approach to veganism if you think it will be the best decision for you. However, since you're new to it, it will begin to seem like a chore and a hard thing to do. So, it is crucial to understand that making this decision benefits you and the environment.

Remember, if a person eats an omnivorous diet for 30 days a month, it equals 90 units of suffering caused in a month because of the three meals eaten in a day. Now, if a hundred people eat the same way, it equals 9000 units of suffering caused by them in a month, which is considered a large amount of suffering. The omnivores worldwide are in the millions, so the units of suffering caused to animals per state or country will be ranked in the millions.

However, if one person in every hundred decides to change their lifestyle and embrace veganism, it will impact the unit of suffering caused per hundred persons. If one person among the hundred persons chooses veganism, the numbers will decrease to 8910 units of suffering. That person's decision has reduced animal suffering by 90 units, substantially impacting for one person.

As a person caring for the stability of the planet and the well-being of all living things, this impact will bring joy.

However, this is not enough to tone down the suffering of animals to a considerable level. The impact of one person's choice is noticeable but barely there.

One vegan choice is just like having ten teachers for a subject. Twenty topics are in the outline; nine teachers come to class and scan through the slides without giving the course a good explanation. Meanwhile, the one who has to teach just two topics comes to class and explains well to the student's understanding. Although the teacher who taught their two topics did an excellent job during the exam, the students will still have problems with the eighteen other parts. This means when they write the exam, although the two topics will help boost their score, it would not have much impact on their grade because they don't have adequate knowledge of the more significant parts.

Similarly, if few vegans stick to their eating routine without faltering, it does not affect animal suffering. This approach is known as the standard approach. The typical approach encourages a person to stick to the vegan eating routine. There is no flexibility in the vegan approach; there is just one eating pattern. The standard vegan diet approach is the step most people choose when becoming vegan. Choosing this common approach might benefit the practitioner but little for animals. The benefits have to be substantial to affect animal suffering. Many people would rather eat their omnivorous diet than choose to eat one pattern of food. Many people want to become vegans, but in all honesty, many people are not interested in the suffering of animals.

That is not saying there aren't people who don't just care. Some people care but don't know how to transition into a vegan diet because of the typical approach. They understand what they need to do, but they can't choose to begin eating green things from the start; it just makes the whole process weird and a lot to deal with. There are many reasons why this common approach does not work.

Why Common Approach Doesn't Work

- **Sudden health problems**

People often wonder why they have health problems after the first few weeks of a vegan diet. The answer is obvious; these people chose the standard approach that ensured they gave up every animal's food. Veganism is a lifestyle, not just one diet; a tough transition into it is bound to cause problems.

To understand this better, think about a child that is consistently given breast milk and needs to start eating other things. Do you see a mother decline to provide the child with milk or forcefully introduce solid foods? No. Even though some people might do that, it is usually because of a lack of information. With adequate information, they would discontinue the practice. Instead, if there is a need to transition from breast milk to other foods, the mother introduces it alongside the breast milk so that the baby does not get overwhelmed.

Similarly, when a new pet is brought home, you don't introduce it to your old pet immediately because it is bound to cause problems if you do it like that. Most pet owners introduce the smell of the new pet to the older pet by letting them sniff the items used by the new pet. The introduction is gradual till the older pet gets used to perceiving the new pet. After the owner notices this, they freely let them play with each other.

Anyone might think this does not apply to adult humans since they aren't babies or pets. Still, it is indeed like this with the human body system. This is why a person who smokes might find it hard to stop smoking, or someone with a bad habit might find it hard to leave. They can quit smoking or the bad habit, but stopping it abruptly might cause many problems. It is similar to when a drug addict gives up their drugs and begins to have withdrawal symptoms.

People who give up their dietary patterns to begin veganism with a typical approach might have gastrointestinal (G.I.) problems. These problems they might have with their gut might be called leaky gut. They get leaky gut because their body is not used to this new pattern of meals, but these fresh meals are the only ones provided to it. There is no sense of familiarity between the body and these meals. It is nutritious but strange since it isn't used to it.

The body has so many compensatory mechanisms to reject a meal that seems foreign to it. The body might use ways like vomiting, diarrhea, and bloating to signal that these foods are new, and it would take a while to adjust to them. This is mainly for people who have consumed tremendous amounts of meat. The gut bacteria responsible for breaking foods in the intestine might be accustomed to doing so with animal-based protein. A swift change to a plant diet might be strange to you, making you take more frequent trips to the toilet than usual. Usually, vegans defecate more than people with other dietary patterns, but it might be extreme initially because of the standard approach.

The new vegan health problems that follow the standard approach are not limited to gastrointestinal issues. Some vegans might face difficulties with energy deficiency and find themselves being weaker than expected by just talking. This is mainly because the body receives lots of nutrients from meat and other animal sources. Since they are new to veganism and take the typical approach, they might not know how to eat to get the energy their body needs to keep up with their lifestyle.

Some people might experience deficiencies in micronutrients like Omega-3 fatty acids, Iron, vitamin B12, and zinc. Usually, a person who does not follow the typical approach to veganism would have learned about the things that are less in plant-based diets and how they can substitute for these nutrients. A person that used to have fish or seafood in meals and turned into strict veganism might have a deficiency in Omega-3 fatty acids over time. Deficiency in Omega-3 fatty acids will lead to dry skin and, in extreme cases, dermatitis.

Similarly, these types of people might have a deficiency in Iron. Most people who have an omnivore diet get Iron from heme-iron found in red meat. Transitioning into a vegan diet using this standard approach will make the body deficient in this nutrient. This nutrient is required to help in hemoglobin synthesis. When it is absent, there are signs like lightheadedness and weakness.

Vitamin B12 and zinc deficiency can be found in all people of all dietary patterns but is most prevalent in vegans. These can be avoided by applying a better approach to veganism, which gives room for flexibility in the initial stages.

- **Mental/emotional exhaustion**

Life stress already accounts for the more significant percentage of the emotional and mental exhaustion people face in the world. Adding a strict lifestyle without proper transitioning will only negatively affect the brain, leading to more emotional and mental health problems.

Most omnivores are used to waking up and making quick meals with eggs and other animal products. It might take time to adjust to ensure they don't go to the store to buy eggs after becoming vegan. It might also be hard giving up a massive piece of steak after years of feasting on steak for dinner. This can cause mental exhaustion because it becomes a chore for them to remember to keep to the new lifestyle.

Since they are new to this lifestyle, they might have to have reminders to keep to this new pattern. Even with the reminders, they might feel lazy to meet these patterns but still want to meet up. A constant turmoil within them might cause them to be mentally exhausted.

Some people might not use reminders to help them remember what they have to eat and might live with omnivores. These people might sometimes forget that they are strict vegans and might consume some dairy or animal products that are not meat. It might be easier to avoid meat, but hard for them to remember other animal products. When this issue of forgetting arises, they tend to wallow in a loop of self-loathe and blame.

They begin to hate themselves for forgetting their new lifestyles. Although they have no one to blame for failing but themselves, it shouldn't be a thing they should dwell over. If they break the streak more than once, it becomes a thing that causes emotional turmoil, especially in people who had had unstable emotions before they chose veganism.

The emotional turmoil continues with each streak broken and each effort to remember their new dietary lifestyle. Continuous emotional crises and mental inconsistencies will lead to exhaustion and burnout. Due to fatigue and burnout, you might see the vegan lashing out more and having more emotional outbursts.

- **Warped with extremist ideology**

Having an extremist ideology is a thing most vegans that took the standard approach cannot escape. Since they took the common practice and experienced some difficulties along the way, they also want new vegans to go through the same experience.

This extremist ideology also makes them behave like they are way on a high horse and gives them an aura of self-righteousness that makes it difficult for people to befriend them.

People with extreme vegan ideologies indoctrinate people into veganism the wrong way. They offend people by the way they talk down on other dietary patterns. The way they feel inside and the lack of conviction in their lifestyle reflect outwardly. These people make it seem like vegans are nasty when they aren't.

These extremist mindsets do have problems not only with omnivores but also with other vegans. Due to believing that they are on a higher pedestal than other people, they brand some vegans dirty. They think that if a person has chosen veganism, they should not eat any plant product that mimics animal products.

The lifestyle they want other vegans to live is challenging because most people transition into veganism from an omnivore dietary pattern. Suddenly not eating what they are used to, they should be allowed to eat meals that mimic the taste of omnivore meals they love. If they have these meals, they would be happier to continue veganism for long periods.

Being warped with an extremist ideology makes it extremely hard for people to coexist with people because they seem like difficult people that are hard to please.

- **Little or no impact on animal suffering**

The impact of veganism on the suffering of the animal population in the world is more effective when there are more vegans. When there are few vegans, they would have an impact on protecting the environment and animals, but not substantially. Since the aim is to eradicate the suffering of animals, more people are needed to achieve it.

The typical approach proves problematic in achieving this aim. Many people love animals in the world; some wouldn't hesitate to bring back a stray animal to the warmth of their home. This is because they have compassion and feel like the animal should have a better life — have food to eat and a roof over their head. Do you think it would be hard for these people to choose a lifestyle that will protect animals? This should not be a lifestyle that should be hard to adopt since they have compassion for animals.

If so, why are there fewer vegans than any dietary pattern?

It is clear that they love animals and desire to protect them and extend protection to the environment, but they dread the typical approach. Many people want to be vegan, but after hearing the rigorous process and all the foods in their fridge they will throw in the bin immediately, they decide that the lifestyle is not for them.

As more people learn about veganism through the typical approach, there will be fewer people embracing veganism. If these people know there are better ways to approach veganism that doesn't necessarily mean punishing your body from the start, they will be happy to adopt veganism. As vegans become fewer, with old vegans losing their conviction because they didn't approach the lifestyle appropriately, the effect vegans have on animal suffering reduces drastically. If a better approach is introduced to new vegans and people interested in veganism, there will be more people adopting veganism. More vegans equal less animal suffering.

Chapter 7
Why Is This The Definitive Method?

In the previous chapter, you can see why the typical approach is not wrong but is not effective in achieving a sustainable, vegan, happy life. A person cannot change their lifestyle drastically and expect to be satisfied. It wouldn't work. Even though they can sustain this new lifestyle for a long time, they will eventually give into the desire to fall back on their previous lifestyle. This does not mean that practice of veganism for a long time using the typical approach is impossible. It is possible, but it is a tricky process that people will prefer to ignore.

This is the reason why a slow transition into veganism is advised. This is not something many vegans will say because they want the change in animal suffering to become positive as soon as it can. However, it is essential to know that every change is gradual and takes considerable time. A sustainable change takes time to complete but can last for several months or even years. This same principle should be applied to veganism.

Just like an addict recovering from addiction will need to gradually replace their triggers with suitable activities, an acholic will be advised to reduce their drink intake till they finally have the grace to willpower to do without. Similarly, a person who wants to become a vegan has to take baby steps to actualize the dream of attaining the fullness of the lifestyle. This is why a definitive method is required when approaching veganism rather than the typical approach.

Definition of the flexible definitive method in veganism

The flexible definitive method is defined as a vegan approach that allows a vegan to practice veganism as flexitarians for a period till they transition into full veganism. A flexible definitive method is the opposite of the typical vegan approach that does not allow for flexibility. This method allows the new vegan to practice veganism flexibly by slowly introducing vegan foods into their diet until they are comfortable becoming vegan. A flexitarian is a person that eats vegan foods while still having an omnivorous dietary pattern.

This method is more effective than the previous methods for several reasons. This method allows you to practice veganism without being extreme. It allows you to practice veganism in a way that will be kinder to your body, emotions, and mental health. This method is a simple method that anyone can do because it is not tasking and does not require you to do much.

YES, YOU CAN START YOUR VEGAN JOURNEY WITHOUT THROWING OUT YOUR FRIDGE!

Even though this statement feels impossible, it is possible. You don't need to throw all the meats, slices of bacon, eggs, and milk in the house because you have chosen veganism – that is a waste and would do nothing short of demotivating you from living a happy vegan life.

What if I tell you the best traditional veganism approach is being vegan one day a week? Wouldn't you be surprised?

Even though it is surprising, you should know that this is the best approach to help you live a happier vegan life.

This approach is straightforward because it does not put you in a straitjacket of living a vegan life, even when you have not found your way around the lifestyle. It helps you practice veganism more simply and flexibly.

The definitive method involves choosing the days you would eat purely plant-based diets. The day you eat vegan foods should be a day that is convenient for you.

You could choose a day that you don't go to work, or you could choose a day that you have busy; it all depends on what will work for you.

Choosing one day in the week where you go vegan makes veganism like a jolly ride or a vacation. It makes the process fascinating. Just like a public or working holiday, it is like a special day for you to halt from the hustle and bustle of the omnivore diet to embrace the newness of veganism.

Remember that it was a trend for people to get vegan detox after years of eating omnivore diets. They were required to eat vegan meals for two to four weeks. Although this is usually tied to health factors, it is a thing that helps some people transition into veganism. The ones that do not transition into veganism begin to see the beautiful side of veganism that they hadn't seen as non-vegans.

Although vegan detox is a way to ease the transition into veganism, this definitive method is still more accessible. It is easier because you won't have to eat vegan meals at a stretch for one week or two before transitioning into full veganism. This process of veganism might take years to transition you into a full vegan because it doesn't focus on speed but on sustainability. Speed is not essential when building a sustainable lifestyle. This means the definitive method is the easiest and the best approach to remaining vegan for a long time.

Depending on you, you can make that vegan day more special by trying out vegan recipes that could work for you. You could go shopping for vegan food condiments, vegetables, and fruits that you consume every week you have your vegan day. Since it is one day in the week, you can use the time to visit a vegan restaurant close to you to learn how vegan food tastes.

Just see that day you chose to go vegan as a day of vegan exploration. You could use it to explore sides of veganism you never knew about; you could try soy-made turkey or chicken. You could try all those omnivore-substitute vegan meals you've always heard of but have never tried. Many people have heard of vegan sandwiches and burgers but think they might not be as good as people say because there is no meat in them. It will be better if you try it for yourself to have a firsthand experience and not just hearsay from those who have had it.

If you think of it, there are a lot of vegan foods to explore, and you'd never know the food that will pique your interest and draw you in till you crave having it every day. Many options are available to you to choose from.

Not to forget the vegan snacks!

Many people will go for omnivore snacks than vegan snacks because omnivore snacks are more prevalent in every mall you go to. Since you have chosen one day as your vegan day, you can use that day to visit malls and check for vegan snacks to buy. Try them, and see the one you love most out of the lot.

During the day you choose, you would have to eat solely plant-based foods without any trace of animal products, including the snacks you eat. Nothing you eat that day should be from animals. If you are convinced about veganism, this is a lifestyle you will be happy about adopting.

Remember, each omnivore meal you eat in a day causes one unit of animal suffering. If we calculate this using thirty days a month and three omnivore meals daily, we will realize 90 units of animal suffering caused by the omnivore. Following this pattern, we will also discover that 21 units of animal suffering are caused per week.

Using this once-a-week approach means that instead of twenty-one units of suffering that would have been caused by eating omnivore meals, eighteen units of suffering will be forced instead. This is quite a significant decrease in one week. It might not be ranking in the tens, but it is good. Reducing the suffering, you cause to animals by three units as a new vegan is a job well done that the environment and animals will be thankful if they could speak in an understandable language. Doing it every week in a month will reduce the suffering you caused to animals to seventy-eight units.

If you compare the units of suffering that would have been caused to animals if you didn't begin veganism and the units of suffering caused by choosing this moderate approach, you will notice that there is a reasonable difference between them. If there are four weeks a month, being vegan for one day each week will reduce animal suffering by twelve units. This is a substantial number of reductions done by one person, which is very impressive.

If you continue this approach for one year, the number will increase, and you will be making a more noticeable impact. This once-a-week approach will make you reduce animal suffering by 144 units. This is above a hundred and not a little impact. If you are consistent, you will reduce animal suffering by 288 units in two years. These numbers might appear small, but if you compare them to the units of suffering you would cause animals if you didn't have this practice, you will understand that the impact is more than you think. You are doing an excellent job for yourself, the animals, and the environment. If you hadn't chosen this veganism, the unit of animal suffering you would have caused in a year would be 1080.

However, since you reduced the yearly unit of suffering you cause to animals by 144, you will be causing only 936 units. This is an excellent reduction in the units of suffering once in thousands. If you had not chosen this lifestyle in two years, you would have caused 2160 units of suffering for animals. However, since you decided to give up three omnivore meals in a week, you would be generating only 1872 units of suffering, which is a significant decrease from the previous numbers of the earlier years.

This will get easy over time, and you might incorporate other days means that you have a substantial impact as a vegan and soon become comfortable with your lifestyle. You might be skeptical about this method working because it seems so easy to practice. You should be assured that this method will work and will be your gateway to full veganism.

This method is best because people will accept it more than other methods. This means that because of the easy method, you might enjoy practicing it with your family and friends. If you have a large family, you can make it work by making it a fun vegan day where everyone goes out to explore vegan options and talk about the things they like about it and the part they are uncomfortable with. This will make the vegan day practice less lonely for you.

This is advised because, as humans, we tend to be more motivated when people around us are doing the same thing. This action of the people around us acts as a stimulus that either spurs us to move or demotivates us. If we have fun with the vegan day with those around us, it may seem like a holiday to look forward to every week.

If this is not a thing your family would like to adopt, you could try it with a colleague or friend to make them join in the fun. As you enjoy it as a fun experience with loved ones, you will less likely forget the day you have set aside to be completely vegan. Even if you fail because of the things on your mind, your friend or family will be there to remind you that you have a day that you should not forget.

Also, practicing one day a week helps you to become comfortable with the idea of being vegan. Many vegans rush into veganism without getting to know veganism on a personal level, which is why most are salty without any genuine reason. As a flexible vegan that practices once a week, you are relaxed and practicing with a calm mental state. This helps you understand various sides of veganism – You learn new terminologies that vegans use, meet, and interact with.

You might not be entirely a vegan yet, but your practice method might also attract other omnivores who might be as curious as you were initially. People are primarily attracted to what seems fun even though they don't understand it. Practicing veganism will attract people to become vegans because they will believe it is a fun way of life. Gradually, as they rehearse and join in the 'fun,' they might get sucked into the lifestyle. This means you are not only saving animals by your once-a-week approach to veganism, but you are also attracting people to save animals by using your approach.

Imagine how many animals will be saved if nine people are convinced to join you simply because they like your approach to veganism. This means that ten people will be making a difference in the animal suffering that will be caused to animals, including you. Suppose ten people are omnivores and have omnivore meals throughout the month. In that case, the unit of animal suffering in a week will be 210 units, making the numbers rank up to 900 units a month of animal suffering. This number excludes the snacks that will be eaten through the weeks in a month. That means average, hundred people cause 9000 units of suffering. This is a lot of suffering caused.

You are correcting these figures and alleviating the burden of animal suffering and environmental pollution by letting your fun vegan lifestyle speak and draw people in. If ten people out of a hundred become vegan, that means that only instead of 9000 units of suffering to be caused in a month 8,880 units will be generated, which is greater than 90 units that would have been caused by one person going vegan in a month.

If these people continue their approach and eventually transition into full veganism, the unit of suffering will decrease. Surely if you start with going vegan for one day, there will be a temptation to add one more day, and the padding will continue till full veganism is achieved. If the ten people begin full veganism, it will be 900 units less animal suffering. This means if 9000 units of suffering are supposed to be caused by hundred people; instead, 8100 units of suffering will be generated. A difference of 900 is tremendous and cannot be ignored.

Also, this method is effective because it allows your body to be used to the lifestyle before full practice.

Chapter 8
A Day Is Not A Day

Since you understand the concept of the definitive approach to veganism and the concept of the average omnivore's meal, you have to realize that snacks are also included in the average omnivore's meal. An average omnivorous meal in a day is made up,

- An omnivorous breakfast includes everything you eat in the morning – the appetizer, main meal, desserts, and snacks. It consists of every non-plant-based diet food you eat in the mornings
- Omnivorous lunch includes everything omnivorous you eat at lunch hour, including the snacks you eat at work, the lunch you buy at the restaurant or pack from home, and the dessert you eat afterward.
- Omnivorous dinner includes everything you eat at dinner time, the main dinner, the appetizer, the desserts, and even the late-night snacks you eat.

These are the constituents of an omnivorous meal; if you give up three average omnivorous meals daily, you must count three different meals. One omnivorous meal could be breakfast, dinner, or lunch, as you choose to go vegan once a week.

You might think that these snacks you eat in a day are not involved in the once-a-week (OaW) thing, but they are. If you choose Sunday as the day you are going vegan because it is a work-free day, you should forget that tub of ice cream in your fridge you devour while binge-watching your favorite series. Also, ignore the turkey you eat with fried rice as a Sunday ritual.

You're also going to give up the milk cookies you bake as desserts; if you can't give it up, you can decide to find a vegan alternative to it. If you don't see or cannot bake anything else, forget about those milk cookies till Monday. You might feel that it is too much to change that Sunday routine of baking those milk cookies. If you need the cookies, you must bake them before your vegan day or afterward. If you bake it while you are on your vegan day, you might have the urge to taste what it tastes like; after tasting, you might notice that you have broken the streak even though you didn't want to.

If this day falls during a festive period when you and your family loves having sweets from milk, cheese, and butter, you will have to stand by your decision to stick to the day you chose.

This method is for people who like following routines to be able to keep up with a new lifestyle. Some people need a good habit to fall back on so that things don't get overwhelming for them. People like this need to stick to the routine mentioned above.

The day you pick does not have to be Sunday; you should select a day that is befitting for you and fitting to your schedule. If you choose a day that is not fitting to your schedule, it becomes more stressful than fun. This process is designed not only for you to transition smoothly into veganism but also for you to have fun alongside. After choosing the day you will be vegan, you can bookmark it on your calendar or your phone. Smartphones have made everything way easier than they were before. If you have a smartphone, you can mark the days in your phone calendar so that it can send you a notification each day you are supposed to be vegan; that way, you will adhere to your practice of veganism.

The way you practice your OaW vegan diet solely depends on the kind of person you are. Remember, the OaW vegan diet subtracts three omnivore meals a week. Subtraction of three omnivore meals in a week is the absolute goal. Hence, it should not matter the way you approach this subtraction; what should matter is that you stick to subtracting three omnivores' diets every week.

Some people might not be fans of everyday living, as much as they would love to practice it one day at a stretch because of convenience and their schedule. These people with a stacked schedule that leaves them no room for adopting a new lifestyle might choose a day in a week. The day in the week they choose does not have to be constant throughout the month. It just has to be perfect enough for you to practice.

You can choose Sunday in the first week since you might be home to try your hand at some vegan recipes. You might also select Friday since it's the last day at work, and you might close earlier than usual. The important thing is doing what works for you.

If the day you chose for the first week doesn't work for you for the second week, you can pick another day. The day does not matter; all that matters is your consistency throughout the process. No matter the day you choose, ensure that you are not tempted with omnivore snacks or desserts. Try to steer clear of things that will make you break the streak. You need to b firm on your decision to be a vegan for a day.

For some people choosing a day where they are vegan are just a no-no and something they cannot stand because they despise routine. If you are a person that falls into this category, don't worry; there is a vegan solution for you.

Since you cannot commit to a day of vegan eating, why not spread the three vegan meals across three days? Remember, the goal of the once-a-week plan is to reduce the average omnivore meal by three times a week. This also means introducing vegan meals and snacks three times a week.

We have twenty-one meals a week: seven breakfasts, seven lunches, and seven dinners. Now, of the twenty-one meals, you can decide which three will be perfect for your once-a-week plan. For a plan that is not carried out in a day, you can determine if you want to plan it before or if you want to wing it as it comes.

If you are a person that would like to plan it, you can decide that every Monday, breakfast and breakfast snacks will be vegan. You could pick the next day, or maybe pick Tuesday's dinner as the next time you would want to eat vegan. For the third day, you could pick Thursday lunch as a day you would like to go vegan, with vegan lunch and vegan snacks. You could choose anytime that will be the most convenient for you because you are the person with the schedule, so you know when it is tight and when it is a bit free for you to practice your new lifestyle. It should be at your convenience, not dictated by someone.

If you prefer winging it, you could just monitor your progress and how well you are doing it every week. You could do it at any time of the week, but ensure that the time you choose, you will not consume anything that is omnivorous, and you will stick to the vegan diet. This process is easy, so it might be easy for you to ignore or handle it with fun. The easiness of this process is motivation enough for you to begin and keep to it as much as you can.

Saying all these might seem a bit strict, but it is not, at least it isn't when compared to the standard approach.

There is no doubt that there will sometimes be when you mess up your routine. As humans, we are perfect but imperfect, so that we might fall short of our expectations.

Sometimes you might see yourself taking a massive bite from a non-vegan cookie from the jar, even though you had announced to yourself and others that you would be eating vegan then. Other times, you might be sad at the time you have set aside for vegan meals, and a cold tub of ice cream is the only companion you need. You might look for the vegan variant but might not find it because not all stores have vegan items even though the lifestyle has gained popularity. Or, the case might not be the stores not having the vegan version but you not having the energy or money to go out to purchase it.

Other times, you might need to celebrate with people and cancel your vegan meal for an omnivore meal to fit in with your friends or family. Other times, you might want to eat something that isn't vegan on the day you have planned to be vegan.

It is okay for all these to happen; this only means you are human and aren't void of imperfection by human nature.

You don't need to batter yourself up about making a mistake eating as an omnivore when you plan to eat vegan. You don't also have to blame yourself for having serious omnivore food cravings because it is normal for people transitioning.

Did you fail to keep your vegan promise to yourself today? Try tomorrow. Failure should never hinder you from trying to live the lifestyle that you want.

If you planned to eat vegan throughout Monday and some surprise meeting came up where you have to eat non-vegan foods and are hungry to endure till you get home, you can also eat. You have to be alive and well to spread the good news of veganism. So, you should do anything to help you care for yourself. Eat the omnivore meal; you can continue the fight another day. Remember, this approach to veganism is flexitarian, not a strict procedure. So, try as much as possible to enjoy it so it doesn't become similar to those practicing strict veganism.

If you planned to eat as a vegan for every breakfast on Friday, and you forgot because you woke up too late, forgot you had work, and decided to throw the closest thing you saw in your mouth, it is okay. You don't have to confine your life to a routine that doesn't suit you.

So, what, because you might miss or forget to remove three omnivore meals for a month, you feel veganism is not for you?

Even the people who are the longest practicing vegans in the world today had times in their lives when they weren't as vegan as they should be. Did that stop them from continuing the vegan lifestyle? It did not.

If you are bent on doing something, it does not matter how many tries you take to achieve it; you will eventually do it. You might fail at it for quite a while; finally, when you understand it, you will be able to do it effortlessly and guide people to do it similarly.

If you failed to do it on a Monday when you planned to do it on Monday, there are other days of the week you can choose from. Monday is not the only day of the week. There is Tuesday, Sunday, Saturday, Thursday, Wednesday, and Friday for you to choose from.

If you planned to do it on Thursday during lunch and failed, there is still Friday and Saturday for you to make up for it.

The important thing for you to know is that beating yourself up about a failed routine in a new lifestyle would not do any good to you. All you need to do for yourself is pick yourself up from where you've fallen and continue from where you stopped. Even though you forget to omit three omnivorous meals in one week, it should not be something disturbing. All you need to do is try to remember the following week. The motivation from the week you failed to keep up with will spur you to keep up with the remaining weeks.

Chapter 9

Sit On The Bank Of A River And Wait: Your Enemy's Corpse Will Soon Float By

It might seem safer to follow the standard approach than this definitive one. After all, many people have used the typical process and are still vegans. Nonetheless, it is safer to use a more straightforward method that will last longer than a strict method with no guarantee of working for everyone. This method has many benefits and guarantees it will work for everyone.

There are many benefits attached to this approach that cannot be overemphasized. These benefits outweigh the doubt about the process.

Benefits of the definitive flexitarian approach to veganism

If you want the best experience during your vegan practice, you should not consider the complex approach or people who try to sway you using the rigid method. Even though these gurus of the standard process say that it worked for them because they are still practicing. Still, the downsides to this practice outweigh the benefits. The benefits of this method are longer lasting and more visible.

There are so many benefits of this approach that, if written, would cover a book independently. For this book only the significant benefits will be tabled in this chapter.

1. It teaches you to be patient with the practice

This might be a surprising benefit for you to see among the benefits this approach brings. Since this practice is at a slower pace than the complicated approach, you will learn a lot of things along the line. One of the essential things you will know from this process is that sometimes you may derail from your lifestyle, and that is okay. It teaches you to take the process with patience. It helps you learn to take it one step at a time. If you have an average tolerance level in your vegan practice, you will have more stable emotions during your transition into full veganism.

Since there were days when you did not eat vegan, you will not beat yourself when you have an omnivore meal after your constant practice of veganism. Following the rigid approach, most people fall short of their vegan practice expectations. When this happens, they rebuke themselves without pity. They do this because there is no process in their transition. They began to be vegan immediately instead of taking one step at a time.

Since they used this method of becoming vegans, they would not be used to having the days that they aren't vegans. This will make them unhappy when they break their streak. They continue to be disappointed because they didn't meet up to their expectations for one day. However, if a person that follows this approach breaks the streak after the transition into full veganism, they will be patient with themselves because of the slow change into veganism. It is more likely that they will not fall short of their expectations after a complete transition because they transitioned healthily into veganism. This patience is a meaningful gift that is important for vegans. This is because there are times when the journey might seem complicated, but with patience, you will have a positive approach that will sustain you as a vegan.

2. **Anyone can practice it**

Another essential feature of this practice is that anybody can practice it without reservation. It is easier than the standard vegan approach, making it easy for every person to practice. The easiness of practice is different from the safety of routine. The procedure's safety is one thing people consider before choosing a lifestyle. This method is safe because it does not negatively impact your emotional, social or physical health. An older person can practice this method as a child can also practice it. This method has no boundaries by nation, age, gender, or economic status. All these boundaries do not exist when practicing veganism using this approach.

Some people who begin a religion might also need to transition into veganism and find it hard to keep to their new beliefs. This method can help them adopt this method that will help them gradually embrace that part of their religion.

Some people might want to practice veganism alongside their children and grow up with a healthy and compassionate lifestyle. Hence, they might want to incorporate these vegan meals into their children's once omnivorous diet. This might be a cause for concern, especially if their children are involved. People tend to consider their lifestyle options more till they know it is safe for their offspring. Some people have changed their children's diet from omnivorous to vegan using the typical approach. It is clear that even those children became vegans since their parents only fed them; it would be a lifestyle that they must have protested against asking for occasional chicken nuggets.

However, with this flexitarian approach, the children might have time to have their favorite meals while still learning what vegan meals are. As they familiarize themselves with eating as a vegan, they gradually get used to vegan substitutes for their favorite meals. Learning about all of these becomes a smoother and easier transition into veganism.

This means that, unlike the typical approach, children can transition easily using this method.

Some people might wonder if veganism is for them because of the nature of their work and the energy it takes to perform tasks. Anyone can become vegan, despite the type of job they have. It is no wonder some bodybuilders will choose veganism as their dietary lifestyle years after discovering their dietary pattern is not suitable for them. Most of these bodybuilders that became vegans testify that they have more incredible strength after transitioning into veganism.

There is no better way to approach veganism as a person with a demanding profession than this. The slow vegan transition allows the person's body to get used to the eating pattern to sustain them for longer.

Since it is easier and takes a slower pace, it is more likely that more people around you can adopt it quickly than the typical rigid vegan approach.

3. Sustainable, successful veganism

It is universal knowledge that slow transition promotes sustainable development. People always say that slow is always steady and is not far from the truth. Most people fear beginning their veganism because they fear it will not last as long as vegans. People hate uncertainty because it puts them on edge when they want to go through the process happily. This reason is why they contemplate veganism for months or years.

Practicing sustainable veganism without being attracted to your previous dietary pattern is possible. However, it might seem complicated to practice sustainable veganism if you follow the cumbersome and common approach.

Most times, the end of a lifestyle is more important than the beginning of the lifestyle. If you care about the future and hope you can be a vegan until you're old and gray, you should only consider using this method. Since you'd be comfortable with the pace of transitioning, you will know when you need to take a break or continue. You would understand the process well, so you tend to practice logically and not just by leading your emotions.

The typical approach will make you act based on your emotions, and your emotions will be more unstable, primarily because of the feelings of frustration you might have within you.

Consider children that were omnivores before transitioning into veganism with their parents. After many years, they often go back to the omnivorous lifestyle because their parents transitioned into veganism using the standard method that does not allow for flexibility. Through this complex approach, they notice that they miss their previous lifestyle, and there is nothing they can do about it. They spend their lives wishing for their previous meals. Due to this, any chance they get, they try omnivore meals.

This means that the approach to veganism affects how sustainable the vegan practice is.

Practicing this lifestyle slowly makes it slowly become part of the person. When a routine is formed, it is hard to back down. The slow practice makes veganism a routine and a sustainable lifestyle. If the typical approach is used, it would be like a chore that you find yourself doing. When a lifestyle becomes a chore, it becomes easy for you to reconsider the correctness of your choice. If you are looking to practice veganism as a long-term thing and not for a quick change, it will be preferable to use this method.

4. It allows you to make little mistakes

Mistakes are engraved in human nature; these mistakes allow us to become better people and know a better approach to problems that we might encounter again. This also applies to veganism because, just like other lifestyles, mistakes are not avoidable in veganism. Sometimes you might do things that aren't vegan, like eating eggs or drinking milk. These are some common vegan mistakes. Some people make mistakes that aren't these. The error of some might be some misconception they have about veganism. Some people about to begin veganism think that veganism is the same as a vegetarian diet.

Sometimes other people believe that veganism gives you adequate nutrients in your meal. So, they become vegan and base their meals on vegan processed foods. This might be hard to believe, but many brands have a vegan alternative to their popular snacks. Many people produce snacks without adding animal products, but are these enough to give you the necessary nutrients? They aren't. These processed foods usually contain calories but have little nutrients to offer.

As a person that took a while to explore all the vegan alternatives before you became a full vegan, you will make these mistakes when you have days that you eat vegan. If the pattern continues, you will eventually realize you are eating unhealthily and have to change. When you transition into full veganism, it would be rare for you to make those mistakes because you have already gotten the hang of the lifestyle. Due to this, these people know refined carbs and their disadvantages and eventually try to avoid them and stick to whole foods.

Another misconception that causes mistakes in some vegans that took the typical approach is eating extremely few calories. They believe that vegan meals are already nutritious, so they don't need to eat much. This most times leads to extreme dieting that some people cannot control. These people become obsessed with eating the same number of calories every day. Eating the same calories daily becomes an eating disorder that makes them lose unhealthy weight.

Some people who aspire to be vegans are afraid of this happening to them, so they pause their decision to become vegan. Transitioning slowly into veganism gives you the time for you to adjust to getting equal calories as you previously got from your previous diet. It allows you to understand how to be vegan without being extreme on your dietary pattern.

You may make many mistakes as a vegan, but the typical approach will not let you be at peace when you make those mistakes because you dived into it wholly from the start. As you practice it slowly, you learn the good things from your mistakes and unlearn your misconceptions.

5. It allows you to try other dietary patterns before full veganism

People say that variety is the spice of life, and they aren't wrong. A life that is full of variety is a life that is full of fun. Imagine waking up every morning to do the same routine for fifty years; you will slowly eat yourself up.

If your lifestyle involves going to work at a particular time and eating the same bland dish, you have consulted many YouTube videos but cannot get one. You still have the same meal at work even though those around you eat lots of fun things. You can eat with them because what they eat goes against what you stand for. If you go home after work and eat the remaining bland meal from the morning, you might not notice that your life has no fun, but gradually you will end up wanting to leave that lifestyle for a new one.

However, if the transition into a new lifestyle is slow, you would have all the time to explore other options without fear of being judged or breaking your beliefs.

If you choose your three AOMs to be in a day because of convenience, you can use the time to explore other dietary options that could be nice for you. You could also explore vegetarianism which is the closest dietary pattern to veganism. You could explore it with the day you choose to go vegan. It would make the transition easier. The nutritional practices you can explore are not limited to vegetarianism or vegan-related dietary patterns. You can also explore pescatarian diets and others.

While you explore these diets, it would be easier for you to learn how to make your future vegan diets fun. You will also know how to make new vegan foods similar to the omnivore diet you love. Gradually, you would find your way around veganism and even create your recipes while trying your hands on different vegan ingredients.

These advantages of flexibility and newfound recipes cannot be achieved using the typical approach. If you use the standard method, you will be like the person in the analogy used in the beginning paragraphs. Happy vegan life is a vegan life that allows you to know that you are not missing out on anything by being vegan. Instead of missing out on something, this traditional approach will guide you till you have the personal conviction to choose veganism because it is the best thing you should do.

6. It builds your tolerance for vegan food

Although a low tolerance for vegan food is not widespread, it still exists. Some people can't stand vegan food. The reason they cannot stand vegan meals is most times not related to allergies, although there are people who are allergic to some plants used in vegan meals. Whatever reason may be why a person has a low tolerance for vegan meals, throwing the person deep into veganism without gradual steps might traumatize the person.

If the person introduced to veganism is a child with no choice but to eat whatever their parent brings to the table, it might be frustrating for the child. Even though they eat a suddenly changed diet, they would not be happy. In cases with low tolerance, they might throw up more often than before to express their distaste for the food they were given. When they do not throw up, they might spend more time in the toilet because their body isn't used to the food.

Truthfully, to begin a new dietary pattern, you need time for your body to adjust to eating in a unique style. It does not matter if you are transitioning into omnivore from a vegan; your body will still need time to get used to the new way you are eating. Every change in diet has to be gradual so that you don't hurt your body or fall sick.

Unlike omnivore meals, whole vegan foods are usually endowed with water and fiber. These vegan meals might not be only fruits but a mixture of fruits and different vegetables, including root vegetables, nuts, legumes, and seeds. Most of these are nutritious but have higher water and fiber when compared to omnivore meals. This might take a while for your body to adjust to digesting these meals. Don't be confused; these meals are readily digested and absorbed by the body, but it might still take time for your body to adjust to get these foods. While the body is taking time to get used to the new meals, the person might have more frequent visits to the toilet than usual.

The typical approach to veganism does not allow a person to get used to vegan meals before complete introduction. Since they go straight into full veganism after being omnivores, their body might take time to learn how to tolerate vegan foods. This does not mean they will be taken to the emergency unit using the standard method. However, it will cause minor toilet problems that can be avoided if another approach is used.

The tolerance level for vegan foods builds over the weeks, months, and years of using this method. Since there is an introduction of three vegan meals every week at first, it is a slow approach but a sure way to let your body understand this plant diet. As time passes, you add one more vegan meal and stick to the four a week while checking how comfortable you are by adding one more meal. The addition goes on till you are satisfied to become fully vegan. You wouldn't even notice the changes in your diet because you have built your tolerance over time.

7. Allows you to learn more about veganism

While practicing the slow veganism approach, you are like a half-vegan. Although you eat vegan meals three times a week, which makes you flexitarian, you can be considered a person who is in-between veganism and an omnivore diet. This means during this period of practicing both; you are part of both diets. This means you can be part of vegan and omnivore groups. You could say you get the best from both worlds during this period. You can use this time to learn about omnivore diets as well as a vegan diets.

Although you might be familiar with many vegan terms since you have been aspiring to be a vegan for so long, that does not mean you know everything about veganism. Practicing it this way makes you learn things as a vegan, not as a curious outsider. There is a significant difference between learning something as part of a group and learning externally as a spectator. As you stand as a vegan, you learn more of the vegan terminologies that you didn't know about. You learn those terms and how to use them.

Vegans are constantly sharing recipes for their meals on social media networks. There are also many vegan recipe videos on YouTube and other social media networks. As a person practicing as a vegan once a week or three vegan meals a week, you can also enjoy these recipes. At least you are a vegan once a week, which means you aren't entirely an omnivore. During this time, you can learn how to explore your options as a vegan in the way that is best for you.

Knowing how to cook good meals as a vegan will only attract you and other people to eat. If the food you cook is tasteless, then being a vegan will be a chore. The people around you will also feel that your decision is pointless. Even though you are particular about the correctness of your decision, it would help if the people around you don't understand.

There are many flavor-filled dishes you can eat as a vegan; the options do not have a limit because you can create your variant of the dish you love. You also learn how to make the most of your dishes during the process. By the time you transition into full veganism, you will be able to relax your tastebuds with different variants of delicious meals.

8. It gives you a chance to practice veganism with social connections with your loved ones

Most people say that vegans are nasty and do not have friends. This is not entirely true, but not false either. Vegans often lose connections with those they love when they begin veganism. This is because they take a complex approach to veganism. Imagine losing the people you connect to because you choose a different lifestyle from the one they knew you had. Most times, the fault is not from the friends or loved ones but the vegan's approach.

Food is a thing people bond over in different countries and different cultures. When a thing that caused a bond between people is suddenly taken away, the relationship will be sour and rocky. Suddenly choosing to stop eating food everyone knows you adore because you want to change your lifestyle can cause a separation between you and those that love you. If the approach is complex, you might have lots of emotional turmoil, which you cannot explain. This might make you unable to explain the reason for choosing veganism. You might know that you made a correct choice, but you don't know how to explain it to others, which might lead to inappropriate outbursts of emotions that can be avoided and unnecessary.

Using the typical approach will make you nasty to people. You might not even be able to be at peace with other vegans because your practice is the best in your eyes. The attitude that might come from the abrupt change might severely affect your social contact with people. Since you delved in deep without testing the waters, you will not be able to attend some gatherings where you need to eat because you can't eat as you could have.

You begin to ignore an invitation to events you have once loved to attend. As you constantly ignore these invitations, you indirectly sever your relationships with several people.

Similarly, eating at public places like cafeterias and restaurants becomes problematic. You can no longer eat with your coworkers during lunch break because you suddenly changed your dietary pattern.

Imagine all these happening at once, and how socially excluded you will feel if it happens. The exclusion does not end with people you know but extends to your routine grocery shopping because not all grocery shops have vegan meal alternatives.

All these are little situations that would have been avoided with the right approach. People that take the traditional flexitarian approach will transition slowly into veganism. As they transition slowly into veganism, they also prepare their social circle for the inevitable significant change. As they chip in that they have a 'vegan' day, the people around them and their social circle will learn how to adjust to make them fit in over time. A true friend will always want to change to fit a friend.

As they adjust, they gradually learn about the shops that have vegan food condiments. As they know everything during this period, they fit right into veganism without reservations or exclusion when they become full vegans. These people who approach veganism this way will have the social capacity to belong to any social circle they desire.

This approach makes it easy to practice veganism with family and friends. It is a straightforward approach that anyone can do, so close people might want to know how the lifestyle is. As you practice eating three vegan meals per week with them, you have one more thing in common and one more thing you can bond over talking.

This method is also helpful to radical vegans who have been practicing veganism for a long. Most vegans became radical by following the typical approach; hence, their views on veganism might b stricter than usual. However, if these radical vegans use this method when explaining veganism to non-vegans, they would want to adopt the lifestyle. These people would have a new view of veganism other than the strict and overly self-righteous they know it for. That will be a plus for veganism if people can see this part of veganism that they didn't know existed.

9. It gives a more fulfilled life during the practice

For several reasons, some vegans are not satisfied with their choice of veganism. The main reason for other reasons stems from contemplating their choice and not knowing how correct it is.

These people practice veganism but mostly feel that they are dragging themselves along the practicing

A person rushes into a lifestyle the same way they might run out of it if they don't understand it thoroughly. The sole way to have a fulfilled life is to know why you are living the life you are living.

This slow and steady method helps you understand why you are a vegan, and the benefits for you, the animals, and the planet it supplies. Since you already have this knowledge, by the time you transition into full veganism, it wouldn't be overwhelming to the stage of traumatizing you. You have already used the diet and the idea that you provide a safer climate for animals and humans. As it is nothing new to you, and you understand everything attached.

At the stage of full veganism, the only thing the person will feel is the fulfillment of having an impact on animal suffering. There will also be fulfillment from being able to practice the lifestyle fully and without wanting to go back to the previous dietary pattern. They are content with their lifestyle and do not consider anything other than that.

As they feel fulfilled, it shows in several ways. One of the signs of this feeling is the ability to share and help people who want to begin veganism. Another sign that a vegan is fulfilled is a vegan being able to express themselves politely when people are curious about the lifestyle. A fulfilled vegan would never start a social media/media war against non-vegans. As a vegan using this gentle approach, you will have a sense of fulfillment that others might not have, reflecting how you handle vegans and non-vegans.

10. It is more fun than the other method

Although no one chooses veganism solely to have fun, having fun once in a while makes life more enjoyable. Since anyone can do this method, you can have fun with your family when you choose to have a vegan day. You can extend the celebration to them to ensure that it is more fun. You can try new vegan restaurants as a group. You can also meet other vegans there. The day you explore as a vegan can also be when you try to cook vegan recipes with your family and friends. You don't have to do great at the recipes; it is okay to cook bland vegan meals first. Although the meals you cook at first might not be all that, the bond you create with your family and friends during that day will be enviable.

There are many ways a person can have fun using this method than the other method. The other method barely leaves room for flexibility; it might be impossible to have fun. This rigid lifestyle makes having fun with friends or family challenges. Its rigidity separates you from loved ones instead of knitting you closely. Since the practice is hard, people around you might not want to adopt it. So, it leaves only you to your vegan practice. You might make some mistakes, but it doesn't allow room for it, instantly becoming a fun killer that no one wants.

It might also be hard to practice because of the tasking nature. Conversely, this flexible method gives you room for exploration. You have the time to explore other dietary patterns before you become a complete vegan. Since the transition is slow, you can make the transition fun by trying things you haven't tried before. As you transition into veganism, no dietary pattern will be strange to you because you have experienced them all. Since you had fun during your transition, you would not feel like you are missing something when you become fully vegan.

How to convince others, thanks to the OaW method

The OaW method is the most effective and best way to approach veganism. Since you have seen the light and importance of this practice, it will be selfish of you to go on without telling people. If it works for you, that means it can work for that family member that has been contemplating a lifestyle change; it can work for that friend that has been curious about veganism but has no willpower to start because of the strictness of the typical approach. It can also work for that coworker who has been interested in your eating pattern but is afraid it is too hard to adopt. This lifestyle can be helpful to everyone around you. Remember, if more people join veganism through your approach, you will create a saner climate for the planet. Each effort you make towards drawing more people into veganism is an effort to lessen animal suffering.

With each person that adopts the lifestyle, you are reducing the animal suffering per month by at least three average omnivore meals. If ten people adopt the lifestyle through you, you are reducing animal suffering by at least thirty units of suffering. The numbers continue going up with each person that embraces the lifestyle. Which brings us to the query, how do you convince others to join veganism using the OaW method? This is a piece of vital knowledge because you need to know the right way to persuade others to join. One vegan cannot impact the world; with more vegans, there will be a substantial impact on various aspects of the world. These steps that will be mentioned in this section will be helpful to you in convincing people to use this method to achieve a more sustainable journey.

1. Lead by example

The best way to encourage people to adopt your lifestyle is to do what you are preaching they should do. No one would follow an activist who does not uphold their activism's morals. Talking about a thing and doing something separate is a sign of unbelief in the cause you are fighting for. If you are campaigning for the destruction of soda drinking, and you drink soda, your message will not be compelling. Your message will seem satirical to a significant number of people.

Many examples can be given because this is an issue many people neglect. If you want people to behave a certain way, you should be ready to show them an example of how it is done if you want them to take you seriously.

If you go to a practical school and the teacher tells you how to create a thing without showing you a similar example, how are you supposed to do it? Even though you have the head knowledge about the subject, you might get confused about the first step to take. This scenario goes in so many situations because people are always looking for examples to follow to make them better and avoid mistakes.

Similarly, if you are encouraging a person to adopt a lifestyle, they need to see that the lifestyle is worth it. There is no ideal way to prove that a lifestyle is good than practicing the lifestyle. You must practice if you want to encourage people to practice veganism using the flexible but definitive approach. You don't have to practice it only when others are there. Practice it even though people are there to see it or not.

It is hypocrisy if you use the flexible approach when people are watching but halt when people aren't. When you practice a lifestyle of hypocrisy, you might forget that you should do what you do when no one is watching in front of people. As you fail and have a slip-up, the people you advise to embrace your lifestyle will lose faith. They wouldn't want to adopt the lifestyle since they believe it is hard.

As you teach them about your lifestyle, they begin to embrace your lifestyle. People are more likely to adopt your lifestyle if you are happy with it and it is easy for you. This means that all your actions as a vegan should point toward how fulfilled you are about your choice. Follow your routine, and don't give up the practice for any reason. As they watch you continually, there will be a longing to adopt your way of life. You don't need to tell them that they can do it too; they have seen the example from your lifestyle that if you can do it, they can do it too.

2. Highlight a gap

If you don't highlight the gap between an omnivore and a vegan diet, some people could not know that there is a difference. There are so many differences in the production pattern and effects of the output on the planets. Some people think veganism is only about abstaining from meat, fish, and dairy products. They do not know that veganism is more than a dietary pattern; it is a lifestyle. Some people might also think veganism is a dietary pattern only motivated by health reasons. Due to their belief that it has to be connected to health reasons, they might not want to practice it because they think they are healthy enough, so they don't need it. There are many details about veganism people do not know. Hence, they believe there is no gap between vegan and omnivore diets.

The gap between veganism and an omnivore diet is so thick and fueled by increased numbers of animals suffering per omnivore. With an increment in the omnivore meal in a diet, there is an increase in animal suffering. The gap is also fueled by the number of carbon gases released during these products' production. The more they are produced and released into the atmosphere, the greater their risk to our environment. The carbon gases released into the atmosphere cause global warming and an abrupt change in the climate of the environment.

There are other things the omnivore diet can bring to our planet, like deforestation, which reduces the amount of pure oxygen we have in circulation. It also causes waterways pollution by releasing agrochemicals into the water, eventually leading to the mass death of aquatic life. There is the extinction of some species because of poaching and overfishing. The gaps in the two sometimes seem enormous but are not discussed.

As you highlight the gap between the two lifestyles, they now understand what it means to be a vegan and why choosing veganism is safe for humans and the planet. As the gap is highlighted, they know there is a gap, and the way to fill it is by taking this approach. As you talk about this, their eyes are open to the suffering caused by choosing an animal-dependent lifestyle.

3. Talk about what you have learned

From this book, you must have learned quite a lot of ways to approach veganism. It would be better for you to share the knowledge you have gained with your friends and family. Although your lifestyle needs to speak for you, it is not always enough time. Your lifestyle might make them want to understand the reason for your choice, but not enough to keep them practicing as vegans for longer. They need to know about what you have learned so that they see things from your point of view and understand you better. People tend to understand other people better if they can put themselves in the situation of those people and understand what the person learned. When they know what you have learned and how you learned it, there is a bigger chance for them to adopt your lifestyle than watching you from the sidelines.

Teach them what you have learned. It is usually exciting to talk about new things with friends and family. As we talk about these things, we tend to feel better when we can share our new knowledge with someone. A sense of satisfaction comes from sharing our ideas and being listened to. The advantage we are considering in this chapter is not the personal advantage but the interpersonal advantage it brings. Teaching about what you have learned makes the knowledge engraved in your mind for extended periods.

There are many things to teach about. You can start by teaching them about the meaning of veganism and what vegans stand for. You can also talk about the average omnivorous meal in the previous chapter. You must have learned many things from this chapter that are necessary to discuss. You can speak about greenhouse gas emissions and other things discussed in the previous chapters. Enlighten them that they can be vegan once a week before transitioning into veganism. Explain that they don't need to follow the complex approach to be valid as vegans. There are unlimited things for you to talk about.

The teaching referred to is not holding literal classes to encourage people to join veganism. If you want that, there is no problem, especially if you have the resources to host many people. The teaching referred to is just talking about veganism. You don't necessarily need to say, "I want you to be a vegan." Saying that will invalidate the person's dietary pattern is not what veganism stands for. Veganism is a lifestyle, as well as other lifestyles that exist.

How people talk about their day and how it went is how you should talk about veganism. Talk about it casually, and chip it into discussions smoothly. As you talk about it, you might get excited that they are willing to listen. Let the excitement flow and watch them be in awe of the knowledge you have gained.

4. Talk about vegan meals you love to eat

Food brings people together, even though everyone in the group does not eat alike. However, the easiest way to separate from people is by criticizing what they eat. One misconception strict vegan has about veganism is that if they make people feel bad about what they eat, they will want to embrace veganism. This is a huge misconception that needs to be abolished. If you tell a person who eats five burgers in a day and has been eating the same number of burgers for five years that they are wrong, do you think they will stop? You can do as much as tell the health implications that will arise if they don't change; they might not change. Instead, what they might do to stop listening to your talk every day is to avoid you.

Talking about the meals a person should not eat can be rude. It does not matter if you say it in the politest voice possible; it can still be regarded as rude. As a vegan, you don't have to make people feel bad about what they eat and how they eat. The goal is to make them see why they should be vegans and not scare them away from practicing veganism. Even though they talk about their diet, don't make insensitive remarks about it. Consider their feelings as much as they will consider yours.

Even though you might be concerned about them, don't make statements like, "Oh, bacon isn't good for you."

If you say they might take it the wrong way, you lose your chance of influencing them with your lifestyle. There are other statements you might say to a non-vegan that might send out wrong signals about you.

"I do not eat your type of food because it is bad for the planet and causes animal suffering."

"At least, I've given up drinking milk; although it doesn't kill the animal, it puts them through tough times."

"I can't imagine having hotdogs anymore."

"Chicken nuggets are overrated."

All these comments seem harmless, but you don't know what they can do to the listener's mind. Some people might not show emotions when you make comments that tick a nerve. Although they might not show emotions, the few things they would think about will be avoiding you or not coming so close to you. Saying these might seem like a good approach to you to draw people into veganism, but it is a terrible approach. It is more judgmental than accommodating. Everyone wants a lifestyle that they feel welcomed in, not a lifestyle that they feel they are judged in. the thought of choosing such a lifestyle can be mentally exhausting.

Instead of talking about what you don't eat and what you despise, talk about what you love. Won't it be nice to hear someone talk about something they love rather than make passive judgmental comments? Everyone indeed prefers the former to the latter. Talk about the new vegan meals you tried when you ate out with a vegan friend. You can also talk about a vegan dish you learned from YouTube and how it turned out well when you cooked it. There are some vegan substitutes for sandwiches; you can also talk about those. If you loved the Tofurkey sandwich, you could also tell them about it. Since you are talking about something you are passionate about, they might want to try those vegan dishes.

5. Sneak in some omnivore-looking vegan meals

People say seeing evidence leads to faith in words. However, when it comes to food, words are not enough to convince people. Many meals have been hyped on the media but turned out to be tasteless but beautiful. Even though presentation matters, taste is the main thing people look out for. After all, they will not taste the presentation while staring; they must put it in their mouth to understand what it tastes like. Although talking about your vegan meals might make them interested in wanting to try them. However, that interest is usually short-lived, especially if they don't taste the food after hearing about it. It is usual for people to forget such essential but little details. Forgetfulness is less likely to happen if they taste the food. If they taste the food once and love it, they would want to have the food multiple times to ensure that they don't forget the taste, even when they don't have the opportunity to have it again.

When you have friends you want to convince to adopt your lifestyle, you can make vegan meals that look like omnivore meals. Remember, when making meals for a person, you must consider their allergies and special needs. You have to know if this person has plant-based allergies; that way, you will know how to regulate the ingredients when preparing. Although it is rare to see people with plant-based allergies, they exist in fewer populations. Most allergies and food intolerance are within the omnivore diet.

Everyone has a meal that they favor. Suppose you have a meal like this that is vegan but looks omnivore; you could learn how to make it. It is easier to gain knowledge about something when you love the taste. Love for a particular food makes people go to lengths to learn to prepare it at home and in the comfort of their home. After knowing how to prepare this meal, you can invite this friend or family over to have a taste of your favorite food. When they come, you don't need to tell them that the food is vegan, especially if you have considered safe ingredients.

After they eat the meal, let them know that what they just ate is not meat but a vegan alternative. They would be surprised that they did not notice the difference. If you cook it to their taste, they might admit that it tastes better than the one they've been having. You could also make them come over by preparing the vegan version of their favorite food. Prepare it so they will love it and ask for more.

If you read this and want to try to make your friends adopt your lifestyle but don't know how to cook, there is a solution for you. If you are not aware of your way around the kitchen or find cooking boring, you can order in. many vegan restaurants allow you to choose the ingredients you want in your food. These restaurants are good at what they do, so it would not be hard for them to mimic an omnivore diet. They will prepare it, so it doesn't have to scream green veggies. Invite this person over to eat their favorite meal that you got from a restaurant. After they realize they have just eaten vegan, they will want to try it more times because of the similarity of taste.

6. Make it a fun activity

It is imperative to ensure that you portray veganism as a fun lifestyle. Many non-vegans perceive veganism as a restrictive lifestyle that does not allow you to eat what you want. They know this about veganism because veganism was harshly presented to them. Since you are bringing this new approach to them, make sure you have fun, too, so they can understand that vegans can have fun. Instead of having three vegan meals at home to cover your routine, why not practice it with people? You could tell them that there is a new restaurant you want to check out and you want company. Before you do this, it would be best to dig into these restaurants to ensure your company will not be disappointed with the food served. Ensure you eat in that restaurant before you take anyone there so you can know what to expect when you take someone there.

While you eat your food, you can chip in on how you practice veganism and how it has gotten more accessible for you over time. They will want to practice or at least learn from you as they eat the food and learn about the fun side of veganism. There are multiple ways you can make your vegan practice fun to entice your friends and family.

Remember the day you chose to be a vegan day for you? You can make them have vegan fun with you that day. As a group, you can explore vegan fast foods and vegan shops or animal sanctuaries. As a vegan also in the process of attaining complete veganism, please explore these vegan shops. As you see new food ingredients you haven't used, buying and trying them out at home with family and friends can be fun. As a group, you can talk about the things you can make with those ingredients that will appeal to the taste buds.

You can also visit an animal sanctuary which is a way for vegans to have fun. Animal sanctuaries are different from zoos. Animal sanctuaries usually put the animals' emotions into mind, creating a safe and lively haven for the animals. Vegans choose their lifestyle because we want the planet to be safer for animals and for animals to live freely without being scared of suffering. When you go to an animal sanctuary, you are least scared of the mistreatment of animals. Seeing the animals is fun and having a chance to make some gestures to them is mind-blowing. You and the person/people with you would be in awe of the majesty of these animals when they are treated properly and given the adequate care they need.

You don't need to only go to restaurants, eat vegan substitutes for omnivore meals, or visit an animal sanctuary to have fun. If you all bond through books, it will be helpful to visit the vegan section of a bookstore; you will find so many fantastic reads. If you are not into reading, then you can have them over to prepare or try to prepare these vegan meals. You could have more fun exploring vegan recipes with those you love by cooking with them.

7. Please don't be angry when they refuse

The mistake many people make is making an enemy out of a person that does not resonate with the way they think. It is the wrong way to think and behave. As you are entitled to your views, so is every person. You are not entitled to force your ideas on another person, as they aren't allowed to do the same. You should only try to influence their decisions, not try to change their lifestyle overnight. It is okay for them not to believe in your lifestyle. If you put yourself in their place and think about what your reaction will be if they are angry because you refused to adopt a lifestyle, you will understand why you should force them to begin veganism if they aren't ready yet.

Although this approach to veganism is the most straightforward method, not everyone will be convinced to believe your words and abandon their previous lifestyle. It is better to have them still close without creating enemies. You have a greater chance to influence them with your lifestyle if they are close to you. No one would want to be influenced by someone they have fallen out with. Keep them close and keep your practice of veganism open, so they can see how easy the practice is for you and how much fun you are having.

If they refuse to be vegan, it does not mean they cannot have fun with you when you are celebrating vegan milestones. You can include them in your vegan fun even if they have made it clear that they would not be vegans. The more you let them see your lifestyle, the more they would have internal wars about veganism. Since change is constant, they might rethink their decision if they see that you are having more fun than them while still being healthy. Your patience with them will determine if they have a change of mind.

Don't think being angry when they refuse is only voicing your anger or showing it in your expression. These are not the only components of anger because you can be angry with a better ability to hide your emotions. Expressing anger is safer than bottled-up anger. Avoiding anger when they refuse is checking your emotions to ensure you don't have extreme bad feelings when they don't do what you want them to do. If you bottle anger because of their refusal, you're bound to let it out in another way that might be unsuitable. You might lash out at them at times you don't expect, or you might transfer aggression to the closest person. These two behaviors will make you seem like a bitter vegan. They might not know you are angry because you want the best for them. Your reaction might cancel you as an ethical person and make you a sour vegan with whom no one wants to hang out.

How a radical vegan can adopt this method when dealing with non-vegans

Radical vegans are the famous vegans everyone knows. These vegans are activists for veganism, with the sole aim of making more people vegans more and reducing the suffering of animals in the world. Their aim is indirectly to bring sanity to the climate and make the planet safer and cleaner. If we consider this objectively, we see that they have many valuable objectives besides their aim. However, people consider action more than the thoughts of your mind. Your aim is usually hidden in your mind, and people judge you by what they see. Even though you have a positive motive and the actions that follow are aggressive, people will rule your motive as unfavorable. Consider having the motive to correct a person's wrong but slap the person in the process. How do you think people will see the person that slapped the other person? Their thoughts will be that the person is violent and needs to face adequate disciplinary measures. No one will initially consider their motive or ask because they went about whatever they had in mind the wrong way.

Similarly, most radical vegans go about their vegan activism the wrong way. They forget they cannot use force or hurtful words to make people embrace veganism. Some of these people might have inappropriate signs to promote veganism. Due to this approach, many people might avoid veganism because of the aggression they might feel it represents. Because some radical vegans lead vegan activism the wrong way, people see vegans as unfriendly and mean when there are so many friendly vegans. If radical vegans change their approach to this method, they will attract more people to veganism and create a better name for vegans.

Radical vegans can use this definitive flexitarian approach to teach people about veganism; more people will adopt veganism. They can educate people on what it means to become vegan once a week and how it will help them. They can begin to educate people on this method without attaching judgment to their words. As they do this without judgment, more people will be intrigued by the lifestyle and try it. They can also bring the facts to the table as they teach people.

As they lay out facts on the planets' benefits and heroic acts, mentioning the animal suffering, they will alleviate more people will be interested. This method is more likely to win people into veganism than the typical method. Using the standard method, they might convince five people to believe in the correctness of veganism. However, the number of people is doubled when this approach is used. If you would have gotten one person to follow veganism the typical way, it might be ninety units of animal suffering you alleviate. Meanwhile, if ten people choose this method, you will reduce animal suffering in the first month by at least 120 units. Another way radical vegans can use this method is to create a vegan day, so many people can eat and have fun the vegan way.

Also, many radical vegans have sour relationships with non-vegans. Sometimes, non-vegans might make fun of your lifestyle because of your approach, but that does not mean that it comes from a malicious heart that wants to make you feel uncomfortable with your choice. Their aim might not be wanting you to change your lifestyle; it might just be casual jesting. It is similar to making fun of a friend that wouldn't stop doing a thing you don't understand. Your motive is just to laugh and have fun with your friend. That is the same thing they might be doing to you. They might want to have fun with you. It is not a joke at your cost, as you might believe. It is just a lighthearted joke that you should take as it is. A bitter person who does not know how to take jokes is a fun killer; people don't like being around them. You can spread the word about veganism faster by being able to take vegan jokes while having fun in your vegan practice. This will make more non-vegans believe that veganism can be a free and fun lifestyle.

Chapter 10
"Once A Week" Is Not Once

If you have applied the method discussed at the beginning of the chapter, you will be eating three vegan meals weekly. Three vegan meals in a week are equal to three AOM less. This should be your new routine for a considerable amount of time. As you practice this regularly, you are trying to form a habit of removing three AOM from your weekly meals. You are trying to form this habit. Habit takes a while to become part of a person. Doing something once does not make it a habit, but continual practice makes it a habit. If you practice this for two weeks, it is not yet a habit. Two weeks equals two days, and six AOM less than would have been consumed. It is not yet enough to think that your habit has solidified, and it is time for you to move to the next level. It can take several weeks if you adapt quickly to lifestyle change, and it can take months if you adapt slowly to a change in lifestyle. Before moving to the next step, you must be sure that eating three vegan meals a week has become part of you. To understand this process, it is crucial to know how habits are formed.

How to create a new habit of three AOM per week for three months

There are several approaches to forming a habit, but the best way to cultivate this new habit and abide by it is by following a slower approach.

- **Create a detailed goal**

You might be a person that desires to wing it without many plans. Even though it boils down to personality, it can be detrimental at the start of your vegan journey. As a new vegan, you must be intentional about the process and detailed. A clear goal presents all the intricacies within. It's not enough to say you will eat three AOM less weekly. If you say that or put that in mind, there is a likelihood that you might not take it as essential. Since it is not detailed, it might not be as important to your subconscious to remember it.

If your plan is detailed, you are making it easier for yourself to act according to your vegan plan once a week. Specifically, a vegan once-a-week approach does not mean you have to do it on a particular day every week. Choosing to do it on a particular day every week should be a thing you do when other days are not convenient. A specific day is more convenient than any reason. For your plan to be specific, you must be specific about how you want to practice veganism. You have to choose if you would prefer to practice it for one day or if you would prefer to practice it on separate days. Although you choose how you want to practice, that is not specific enough to keep you going.

If you decide to practice your veganism in one day, you have to choose a specific day in the week that is convenient for you to practice. If you choose Monday, you must stick to Monday until the end. So, it is essential to consider all the factors involved before choosing a day in the week that is suitable because you will stick with it for longer.

If you decide to share the three AOM less meals over three days, then you have to be specific about the days you will spread it across. You can choose Friday, Saturday, and Sunday if the weekend is more leisurely. The specificity of your plan shouldn't end here because you need to make it specific so you don't leave room for mistakes. On Friday, you should choose if the vegan meal you will eat well at breakfast, dinner, or lunch. The same method should be applied to other days. If you choose dinner on Friday, you will eat a vegan meal every dinner on Friday. Similarly, if you choose Sunday and lunch, each lunch you eat every Sunday has to be vegan. It does not matter the three days you choose; what matters is that you are specific about the plan.

Choose days that are close to each other so that they can be easy for you to remember. If you choose days that are not close to each other, you should be sure that they are days you can easily remember. If you can remember to do it on the same day and same time every week, then you are good to go. The more specific you are, the more accountable you are in your journey.

- **Use the help of a reminder**

It is not enough to make your goals specific, specificity makes your goal more critical and makes you strive to achieve it, but it might not remind you. It would be rewarding to remember to keep up with your routine to make it a habit. Remember, a routine is different from a habit. Doing a routine does not mean you will remember it or want to do it all the time. Although a routine is an essential factor when forming a habit. Still, there are times that you might forget to do your routine. An example of a routine is doing the dishes after eating. It is a routine, but sometimes you might forget or procrastinate on purpose. You'd be happy to find someone who would fulfill your dishwashing duties. However, if it is a habit, you will never forget it and wouldn't want anyone to do it for you.

Since the OaW method is not yet a habit, you should use a reminder that will remind you. Smartphones have made it more accessible in this age, so you can easily set a reminder on your calendar app for the times of the month you will practice veganism and free times. You can use many apps to set a reminder, so you don't forget to keep up with your routine.

Some people keep to a routine more when a person rather than a device does the reminder. If you have a friend or a family you stay with, they can remind you on the days you agreed to be vegan. However, if you know that they are not reliable in this aspect, it will be helpful for you to stick with the reminders on a smartphone. Humans forget a lot; if you forget, the other person might also forget.

It would be best if you remembered to keep to your vegan practice because unless your routine is continuous, you might not build a habit. If your routine is constant through your practice, it means that your routine will become a habit sooner than later. If you break the streak multiple times, there is a chance that you might become tired of your routine and give up.

- **Make it enjoyable to repeat**

It is easier to stick to the behavior you find interesting. Consider two options, doing dishes immediately after breakfast and watching your favorite TV show at a specific time every day. The first is a routine you cannot do without. If you go days without washing the dishes in your house, it would be because you have someone to do them. If there is no one to do them, and they lay in the sink for days and weeks, you will eventually have to do it or throw the plates away. Washing the dishes is mandatory but no fun most times, so we would instead procrastinate or hope another person does it. The second option is a leisure activity that might not substantially impact our lives, and we can survive without it. However, we would stick to it, even though we have other things to do. We find the show interesting, ensuring that we watch it every day.

Considering the two options, it is clear which one is a routine and which routine can quickly become a habit. The first option is a mandatory activity but no fun, so it stays as a routine. The second activity adds nothing to our lives, but we would rather have it because it is fun and we like it.

If we apply this principle to the OaW vegan approach method, we would understand that if we make our vegan routine boring, we would easily stray from the goal of veganism. Instead of our lifestyles being like watching our favorite TV shows, it would be a chore that we have to do, but deep down, we know that if we could escape it, we would escape it. If you have a boring vegan routine, you will drag yourself every vegan day without motivation, like a person forced to accept a lifestyle they cannot keep up with.

You can have fun by having a different vegan meal each week. Doing this is exploring the different vegan meals. You can choose to order the meals or cook them yourself. When you do this, you will look forward to every week's vegan day because there will always be something new for you to try.

In the previous chapters, there are highlights about how you can have fun as a vegan. Since the journey is about you before putting others into consideration, those vegan exploring activities you might have with friends and family can be used personally. Make your veganism so enticing to yourself that it is the thing you look forward to every week.

- **Don't break the streak unless the situation is not under your control**

In the second bullet, the idea was to have a reminder to avoid breaking the streak. Breaking the chain of the practice of a routine can be detrimental to a person. Consider a person about to build the habit of taking out the trash daily through the routine. This person would have a routine of throwing the garbage into the waste bin outside every night. Since it delays forming a habit, it might take a while for this person to do this task effortlessly. If they miss their routine for a day because of a flimsy reason, there is a chance that they might miss it again, except they have a firm resolution not to miss it. As they keep missing their previous routine, they eventually give up taking the trash out. Taking the trash out no longer becomes a routine but something they do when they can remember or something they hope that someone will help them with.

Similarly, if you miss practicing your three AOM less per week for no reason, you might set yourself up to miss more weeks. The gap between the day you missed and the next day is seven days. The seven days gap represents one week gap for you to forget your routine. It is important to remember there was one week leading to the day you avoided your routine and one week after leading to the day of your next practice. This gives a total of two weeks, enough for you to forget to carry on. However, if you are resolute, you might keep up with the following week. If you take it with levity, you might forget the next week, which makes it three weeks of forgetfulness. This gradually pulls you away from your vegan routine.

This does not mean you should stick to your routine if an unfavorable situation arises. If unforeseen circumstances come, you must do what needs to be done. Since you are committed to your routine, you will want to replace the day with another day in the week. This means that the process is vital to you, and you would stick with it if not for unfavorable circumstances. Since you broke the streak because circumstances weren't within your control, it might not count. If you ate an omnivorous breakfast meal on Friday for whatever reason, you could move the vegan meal to lunch or dinner, as it suits you.

- **Reward yourself when you keep up with the routine**

Remember how you give your dog treats for being a good boy, and it does the same thing it did to get the treat? This behavior is the same in humans; we are drawn to things we benefit from. If there are two actions we need to take and we would benefit from one more than the other, we would choose the one that is more beneficial for us.

Don't be a stranger to yourself; make your vegan journey worthwhile by achieving milestones. If you have goals that are in milestones, when you achieve a milestone, applaud yourself. You might not necessarily reward yourself with a new cloth or a new item, but acknowledging that you have done well by achieving that milestone is enough.

However, if you have the resources to reward yourself with material gifts, you can. When you reward yourself, you give yourself something to look forward to. You will be eager to achieve that milestone to reward yourself. It might make you more steadfast in your new journey to veganism.

If you don't know how to reward yourself, you can try journaling your accomplishments as a vegan. Those things that seem hard that you accomplished are essential to write down. You will learn to appreciate yourself more as you write down all these accomplishments. Self-appreciation and gratitude are chief motivators that people ignore. If you can appreciate yourself more, you will attain greater heights than you are now. Also, self-appreciation will give you positive thoughts about your lifestyle, which will help you maintain it.

- **Find like minds that can be a support system**

It is okay to start and continue your vegan lifestyle alone, but it is even better to have people like you around to support you in achieving your goal. As much as you should stay with like-minded people on your journey, you shouldn't do away with your omnivore friends who do not have the same motives.

If you can help your friends learn more about your lifestyle, they might want to join you. As they join your lifestyle, you will notice that practicing is more fun. If you start simultaneously, you can make it a competition. The winner will be the winner who keeps the streaks and achieves less AOM than the other. If you don't like that way, there are other ways for you to make it fun with your friends. You can explore the vegan side together and visit vegan restaurants and animal sanctuaries. You can do anything fun for yourself.

If the company you find as a support system has been a vegan longer than you have, it can motivate you when you get tired of keeping to your belief as a vegan. Since they have experienced veganism before you and they know how it was when they began, they can offer valuable advice to you to stabilize you in your vegan journey. They might also have enjoyed the fun side of veganism, so they can lead you through the parts you don't understand.

These people are not only there to have fun with you and show you the way. Sometimes you might hit a rock and become disappointed in following the lifestyle. At these times, you would need support from people who genuinely understand what it means to be vegan.

These people will be able to give you support and advice as fellow vegans.

Signs show that our past month's routine is now a habit.

If your routine is now a habit, you can safely move on to the next step. Below are the signs that will show you that your routine is now a habit. If you notice that you experience these signs, you have to move on to the next step.

1. You feel uncomfortable when you don't do it

If a routine has not become a habit, we would always think of the sacrifice we are making by doing the routine. If we have someone to alleviate the routine and stand in our place, we will be happy. Also, if there is news that no one should embrace veganism anymore, we might be happy because that means we get to go to our previous lifestyle.

However, if this routine of eating three AOM less in a week is now a habit, you would do it without thinking. It has become a lifestyle for you. It is just like eating every day, you do it effortlessly, and when you don't, it is weird or because of a serious reason. Similarly, when the OaW method is a habit, you will be uncomfortable when you don't do it. It is now part of your life; you don't exist independently apart from it. You are joined with it, and it is weird when someone asks you not to do it.

2. You don't fret about forgetting it

Fear of forgetting is attached to the probability of forgetting. If you have a routine, you might be afraid of forgetting or breaking the streak. To keep up with your routine, you might set a reminder that will remind you when it is time. You do this to remind yourself, so you don't break the streak. This is because you are unaware of yourself and your power of remembrance. Even though you might remember, you are afraid of forgetting and losing focus on your practice. If your routine is now a habit, you will effortlessly do it. You would see yourself doing it without reminding yourself or someone reminding you. Since you would do it without forgetting, there would be no fear of forgetting.

3. It is no longer an accomplishment to stick to it

Remember, at the start, it was advised to reward yourself when you stick to a milestone in your routine. The practice of rewarding yourself is to encourage you to stick to your lifestyle more. Since you are a beginner, every accomplishment in the journey, however, when you have formed this routine as a habit, you will no longer need to reward yourself when you stick to it. It is your lifestyle, so seeing it as an accomplishment each time you do it will be weird. It is similar to seeing drinking water or eating as an accomplishment. Even though they might be things worth being thankful for, they are habits even a child has from three years. Eating is not an accomplishment but part of your lifestyle and something you do to survive. Similarly, when you are used to your lifestyle, it is expected that you wouldn't want anyone to applaud you.

4. You don't need motivation

Most times, people need motivation when they have to do a routine. Like a person picking up a liking in a sport would want to be motivated to begin training for that sport. On the other hand, a person who has practiced that sport for more extended and loves the sport will see themselves in the gym or the practice field every morning practicing. In the initial stages of the OaW journey, you might need a slight push from those around you and other vegans to keep to your practice. You will practice it like it is just breathing when it is a habit. It will be effortless. You would not find yourself halting between a vegan and an omnivore diet the day you have set to be vegan. You would wake up and prepare the type of vegan meal you want or order a vegan meal from your favorite restaurant. It is expected, so you don't need anyone to tell you what to do.

5. You only miss a day when the situation is out of your control

Everyone likes to stick to activities that bring joy rather than any other type of activity. When the OaW method is a habit, you will be happy to practice every week. As you have set your goals, every day you have set to eat vegan, you will keep it. If you miss a day, it will either be because of sickness or other extreme conditions. As you miss that day, you will be so uncomfortable and wish to replace that day with another day so you can be at peace in your mind. If you miss the day of practice effortlessly without feeling within, then the OaW has not become a habit. If you miss a day and aren't uncomfortable, it is a sign that you need to continue the OaW until you get used to it.

6. It is fun

If a routine is a habit, you will be happy to do it. It does not feel like a sacrifice or a restrictive lifestyle. It is something that is part of you, something that brings joy to you. If the OaW method is a habit, you will be happy to do it every time. Even though it might seem like a bit of action or something people do not place value on, you would have fun while doing it. Anytime you do it, there is a joy that you have completed your life. You would be surprised how a thing you don't consider tangible can cause you sadness once you do without it. If you notice this when practicing the OaW approach, it should sign that it is time to move on to the next step.

What is the next step?

Through this process, you are now stable in your practice of veganism. It is more of a regular thing than a sacrifice. Remember, at first, you joined veganism because of your motive to create a safer planet for everyone. At first, the motive behind your mind is the sacrifice to ensure you are doing the right thing. You are sacrificing those omnivore meals you enjoy tasting to ensure that animals are safer. As time passes, it is no longer just a sacrifice but a way of life — it is normal. It is no longer a big deal for you to eat three AOM less than usual. As this OaW is now a habit, you will be able to take the next step quickly. When you see the signs that it is now a habit, you must move from once to twice a week.

It is imperative to avoid rushing the process immediately after you succeed at your first milestone. It might be tempting to go from eating vegan once a week to eating thrice a week. Don't heed that temptation because it will not do you good. Just as you gave yourself time to make the OaW approach a habit, be patient with yourself in the second step. Eating as a vegan two times a week means eating six AOM less weekly. It is okay if it takes you months to become acquainted with adding one more day because everyone has different times to become used to a behavior. After you get used to the second day, move on to the third day. Repeat this process till you are entirely a vegan. Don't worry about the time it takes to attain full veganism; the important thing is that you have already embraced the lifestyle, and you're moving towards immersing yourself wholly in it. It might take some people a season to achieve veganism using this method, while others might take one, two, or three years. It all depends on how quickly you adapt as a person.

Chapter 11
Action Creates New Awareness

Using this approach will create more awareness surrounding veganism. People will understand that there are other ways toward veganism than the complicated approach. This book shows that the OaW approach is the only sustainable approach to beginning veganism and cannot be compared to any other method. The drastic approach is problematic and poses many problems to the practitioner.

If you want to be intentional about your vegan journey, this is the path you need to take. This approach resolves all the problems associated with the drastic approach. The OaW approach bridges the practice of veganism and the process of practice. The problems involved in the drastic approach are diluted in this approach.

The three main problems highlighted in the previous chapter, as the consequences of the drastic approach, are erased with the use of this approach.

In this approach, lack of willpower is blurred from the scene. Usually, the problem of lack of willpower comes when you need great effort to carry out a task. Think of when you had an arduous task to handle and how you procrastinated. If there is no one to motivate you to do it, you continue procrastinating till you find the motivation within. Conversely, if you have an easy task to handle, like eating, even though you don't feel like doing it at the moment when you want to do it, you don't need anyone to motivate you. Little efforts require little willpower.

If the effort needed to perform a task is continually reduced, then the willpower needed will also be diluted. Using the drastic approach in your vegan journey makes you struggle and put in much effort. However, you do not need to struggle using the once-a-week approach. Having no struggle is equivalent to not needing the willpower to perform the task. A person who uses this approach will practice it effortlessly, without internal battles and fighting their minds like enemies.

Negative external stimuli, which is a problem for most people that follow the drastic approach, will not be a problem for people that follow this approach. This is because negative external stimuli come from abrupt changes that they don't understand and are unprepared for. This is the most manageable problem to be eliminated among the other problems. Since you will be vegan once a week and are afraid of receiving negative feedback from people, you can decide not to tell them. Since the change is small and limited to three fewer AOM per week, you can continue your social and family life without anyone noticing. It will be needless to despairingly skip family lunches and business dinners because of fear of comments about your lifestyle. No one will notice anything, so that they won't comment. If your vegan day clashes with the day you will eat with nonvegans; you can move it forward. It is a personal lifestyle; it does not need to counter your social life.

Loss of self-esteem, which might ensue from the drastic approach, becomes a fear of this approach's past. This loss of self-esteem stems from the failure to achieve one's goals, as specified in the previous chapters. A sense of achievement stems from sticking with your change program. If you choose a method for a lifestyle that works, you will be motivated to stick to it every week and every month. It makes you lose the fear of criticism because your approach is working, and you have evidence that it is working. This is a booster of self-esteem and moods. You will be happier to continue because it works for you, and you are confident in the process.

Conclusion

If It Worked Once, Why Couldn't It Work Again?

The method has been explained in all the previous chapters, and the easy steps to take to achieve maximum results. As you understand it, don't delay starting to become the person you want to do. Delay is very detrimental to every critical journey. The knowledge gained might gradually be forgotten if you don't use it. If you delay starting this journey, you might lose the motivation you might have after you have read the previous chapters. If you delay, you are doing no one but yourself. It would help if you began this immediately after reading this book. You have all the tools to begin this journey. To begin this journey, you don't have to be a billionaire or millionaire. The important thing you need to begin with is the knowledge you gained from the previous chapter. No obstacle is insurmountable with the knowledge you have gotten. All that is unresolved is for you to put this knowledge into action. Thinking about veganism or having knowledge of veganism does not make you automatically start. You have to start, and the first step is making your goal specific. You don't need physical tools to make your goal specific. All you need is to be deliberate about the person you strive to become.

Although you are making veganism easier for yourself by choosing this method, it does not mean you would not experience problems.

No venture in life does not have problems. In every aspect of life, you will experience problems, but knowledge will equip you to overcome the problems.

Experiencing obstacles along the way is normal and shouldn't be a reason for you to give up. Sometimes, these challenges help you be a better version of yourself. If you look beyond complaining and analyze it according to your gathered knowledge, you will understand that these problems have pointers to their solution. Be patient whenever you get to a point where you think you can't continue. Don't give up; if it gets too tedious, you can speak to people who have been vegans for longer; they can be a support system.

Remember, you are not becoming a hundred percent vegan immediately, so there is nothing you are afraid of. The once-a-week approach makes you become 14% vegan at a time. For a vast lifestyle like veganism, fourteen percent is enough for starting – it can be considered a good start. You get to be fourteen percent vegan seven times in a year or two. The process is straightforward. You are going through seven steps. It is not wrong that the first step takes longer than the other steps. The first step might take three weeks or two months, or more. Be patient because the following steps will not take as long as this one. The other steps after the first might take shorter because you are already accustomed to the lifestyle. Adding more days to your lifestyle does not make much difference. By the time you get to the third step, you will already be 42 percent vegan. That means within a year; you would be almost half a vegan. If you build habits fast, you might be 56 percent vegan within a year, which means you can attain four steps within a year. It is also okay if you cannot attain it within a year because everyone has a rate at which they form habits. Whatever time it takes, you need to be patient with yourself.

Role of the OaW in your life

The OaW method is not only valuable for beginning veganism; you can apply this method when adopting any healthy lifestyle. When you are a vegan using the OaW method, it teaches you patience, which you can apply to other lifestyles. Many people find it difficult to change their lifestyles because they want a quick change. A quick change is primarily unsustainable and unstable. You might experience a quick change, but there is no guarantee that this change will be present for longer. No lifestyle cannot be changed if you take this slow approach. All you need is patience with yourself and with the process. Even medical treatments require some time to take effect in the body.

Why not test your change capacity by applying this method to other areas?

What if I told you, you could be a better version of yourself once a week?

You can become that person you have dreamt of being by trying once a week.

Some people might want to quit smoking and drinking but might find it hard because of the consequences of withdrawal. If you are a person in this condition, you can decide to quit smoking and drinking once a week. If you stop drinking and smoking altogether at the start, you might have a relapse, and it might be frustrating for you to deal with. Instead, you can plan the day in the week that you will strive to ignore the temptation of smoking a stick cigarette or taking a shot of alcohol. Just like veganism, if you get used to it, you can move on to incorporating one more day. As you go on, you can add one more day till you are free from alcohol and smoking.

You can also apply this method to losing weight or getting in shape. It might be hard to get up and exercise every morning or evening, but like the other steps, you have to plan how you want to exercise and the day you have chosen to exercise. It might be hard at first, but find like minds, and ensure you have a reminder to practice it every week. When exercising once a week has become a lifestyle, you can add one more day till you gradually get to the point where you exercise at least three times a week. If you have a problem with drinking lots of water and eating right, you can start once a week. On the other days, you can drink water and eat whatever you like, but on the day you have chosen, you have to eat healthily and drink lots of water.

You can also fight anxiety once a week. During this time, you can make conscious efforts to understand what makes you anxious and try mind relaxation exercises. Gradually move these exercises to a higher notch by adding another day. You can also fight procrastination once a week by choosing a day where you will do everything you have to do without relegating it to the background. If you have a journal to write in, you make an entry on that day. You can choose that day to remember the responsibilities you have forgotten. Keep up with this routine, and eventually, you will be able to stop procrastinating and attend to your duties on time.

If you desire to spend quality time with your children, you can start once a week. Even though you are used to spending time away from them, you can begin to get close to them once a week. When beginning the process, you can draw out activities you will do each day you spend with your children. Choose a convenient day that you can spend time with your children. After this has become a habit, it will become part of you to do it without reservation. You can move on to adding one more day to your practice.

You can also use this method if you find it hard to save money. You can cultivate the routine of saving money once weekly; eventually, the routine will become a habit, and you will not be happy if you cannot save money. Another problem people find hard to eliminate is leaving their smartphones alone. People even use smartphones to get rid of anxiety. However, it is unhealthy to continue using smartphones for prolonged periods. Sometimes, it is good to do without smartphones and connect with the real world. If you have problems leaving your smartphone alone, you can use this OaW approach. You can get a flip phone to make calls with on the day you are not using your smartphone. If you continue this practice for a long time, you will eventually be able to do without your smartphone.

You can apply this topic to several areas of life, and you will succeed in all if you practice it according to the book's guidelines. Many areas are not covered because of the size of the book but will be tackled in other publications.

If you like this method and it worked for you, don't forget to spread the word about it. You can lend it to your friend or family who might need it or recommend it to them for purchase.

Visit www.saturneditors.com/bradmeier